A TV Guide to Life

HOW I LEARNED EVERYTHING
I NEEDED TO KNOW
FROM WATCHING TELEVISION

T0339980

JEFF ALEXANDER

B

BERKLEY BOOKS, NEW YORK

THE BERKLEY PUBLISHING GROUP
Published by the Penguin Group
Penguin Group (USA) Inc.
375 Hudson Street, New York, New York 10014, USA
Penguin Group (Canada), 90 Eglinton Avenue East, Suite 700, Toronto,
Ontario M4P 2Y3, Canada (a division of Pearson Penguin Canada Inc.)
Penguin Books Ltd., 80 Strand, London WC2R 0RL, England
Penguin Group Ireland, 25 St. Stephen's Green, Dublin 2, Ireland
(a division of Penguin Books Ltd.)
Penguin Group (Australia), 250 Camberwell Road,
Camberwell, Victoria 3124, Australia
(a division of Pearson Australia Group Pty. Ltd.)
Penguin Books India Pvt. Ltd., 11 Community Centre,
Panchsheel Park, New Delhi—110 017, India
Penguin Group (NZ), 67 Apollo Drive, Rosedale,
North Shore 0632, New Zealand (a division of Pearson New Zealand Ltd.)
Penguin Books (South Africa) (Pty.) Ltd., 24 Sturdee Avenue, Rosebank,
Johannesburg 2196, South Africa

Penguin Books Ltd., Registered Offices:
80 Strand, London WC2R 0RL, England

The publisher does not have any control over and does not assume any
responsibility for author or third-party websites or their content.

PRINTING HISTORY
Berkley trade paperback edition / July 2008

Library of Congress Cataloging-in-Publication Data

Alexander, Jeff, 1970–
A TV guide to life : how I learned everything I needed to know from
watching television / Jeff Alexander.
p. cm.
ISBN 978-0-425-22155-6
1. Television broadcasting—Social aspects. I. Title.

PN1992.6.A36 2008
302.23'45—dc22   2008000482

147204767

For Lora and Max

CONTENTS

CONTENTS

Introduction

If they are right, and this instrument is good for nothing but to entertain, amuse and insulate, then the tube is flickering now and we will soon see that the whole struggle is lost. This instrument can teach, it can illuminate; yes, and it can even inspire. But it can do so only to the extent that humans are determined to use it to those ends.

David Strathairn as Edward R. Murrow in
Good Night, and Good Luck
Aired on TV at some point

Remember what your parents used to say to you about watching too much television? The exact words? Of course you don't, because they weren't spoken by famous actors in a funny way. But the gist was probably that it would rot your brain.

So is it true? Does television really rot your brain? I think not. I've been watching television my whole life, and cataloging all the things I've learned at the cathode ray teat would be a Herculean task. But with this book, I'm going to try. Perhaps now you're challenging me to name one thing that television has actually taught me. Well, I can tell you the first thing I learned from TV. I was three years old when television taught me how to read.

Ever since the crash-course trifecta of *Sesame Street*, *Mr. Rogers' Neighborhood*, and *The Electric Company* ushered me into literacy, television has taught me everything I need to know, from vital facts about physics and the world we live in, to the truth about interpersonal relationships between coworkers, relatives, friends, and lovers.

(Wait, I exaggerate. There was about a year and a half when I didn't own a TV. During that period I was underemployed, poor, depressed, and not getting any smarter.)

Not all that long ago, there wasn't any TV at all, and the way most people had to learn about the world was by becoming apprenticed to a tradesman or artisan at an early age. This form of indentured servitude was ideal for teaching the next generation of silversmiths, coopers, cobblers, and what have you such valuable skills as making silver, barrels, shoes, and what have you (not to mention exactly how the previous generation of silversmiths, coopers, cobblers, and what have you took their breakfasts). But it taught them nothing about the wider world, things they might have needed to know if they were ever called upon to, say, marry women completely out of their league, or operate a defibrillator, or determine whether a person of their acquaintance was an evil robot. Fortunately, we now have a more wide-ranging, comprehensive, and generally accessible system for disseminating general knowledge, and its initials are *T* and *V*.

Keep in mind, I'm not just talking about what's known as "educational" TV. Of course it's no secret that there's a great deal to be learned from public television, not to mention cable channels further up the dial that have words like *Health* and *Discovery* and *History* and *Geographic* and *Food* right in their names. Gleaning lessons from those channels doesn't take any work at all. They sound like a junior high schedule, for Pete's sake.

Therefore, I plan to avoid the "educational" genre almost altogether in this book.[1] So no "learning" programming (too didactic), talk shows (too dry), soap operas (too slow), cooking shows (how do you know if yours tastes right?), or reality TV (those people are fucking insane). And yes, you could probably pick up a lot from watching the news, but these shows tend to assume that you come to the table with a lot of preexisting knowledge, like who the current President of the United States is and so forth. Since that job changes hands at least once on any given season of *24*, it's kind of a lot to keep track of.

Consider instead the shows that have been entertaining, amusing, and insulating (to use Murrow's downerish words) for the last half century or more. Murrow (or at least David Strathairn) said that learning from television is only possible if we're determined to use it to those ends. Not even a game show can compare to the rate at which fictional, scripted television is able to scoop knowledge into your skull—if that's what you want it to do. And what shows more determination than resolv-

---

1. Obviously commercials can be highly instructive as well, but they tend to have a rather narrow focus, not to mention an obvious agenda. From them we know that Brand X is the best. And we also know that Brand Y is the best, which tells us right off the bat that the concept of "best" can be highly subjective. As if the Emmys hadn't told us that already.

ing to master physics by watching episode after episode of *The Dukes of Hazzard*?

Some philosopher or another (I'll tell you which one as soon as somebody makes a TV series about him) posited that in theory, it's possible to sit alone in a dark cave for your whole life and accurately deduce everything about the world, humanity, and the nature of existence itself. And maybe it is. But it would probably go a lot more quickly and be loads more entertaining if you had a fifty-two-inch plasma in there with you.

So what if television isn't always an accurate reflection of reality? That doesn't mean it can't teach us things (besides what stuff to buy, I mean). Yes, television has certain limitations, but then so does any other art form. Painting, music, theater, writing, dance, scrapbooking—they all have their specific vocabulary, shorthand, and conventions. And if you've ever been to a *Star Trek* convention, you know what I'm talking about.

I'm not going to lie to you. In the University of Television, with hundreds of channels going 24/7, and some channels going back over fifty years (even though it was more like 12/6 back then), I've skipped a lot of class. There's just no way to have seen it all, even with reruns. But over a lifetime in front of the tube, I've been able to synthesize certain themes and ideas that have stood the test of time. The bottom line is that television—regular, noneducational, prime-time TV—can pretty much teach you all you really need to know to get by in the world.

And if we impose certain subject-matter limitations on ourselves for the upcoming lessons, we'll notice that it leaves a much lower percentage of total airtime than there used to be. First-run dramas and comedies are being slowly replaced by reality programming and prime-time game shows. Reruns are becoming a thing of the past—not only in prime time, when the networks trot out crappy summer replacement series and more reality shows—but during the day, when the spots that used to be devoted to reruns of *Barney Miller* and *Bewitched* have been given over to talk shows, infomercials, and fake courtrooms presided over by madpeople. In short, airtime is running out, and we've got to learn from TV scriptwriters while they're still around. After all, people thought the apprenticeship model would be around forever, and even the Donald Trump version of that is just about on its last legs now.

Even so, learning about the world from television is like drinking from a fire hose. You need someone to organize it all, to guide you through the confusing flood of knowledge that pours into your house every time you hit your remote's on button. That's where I come in.

I'm thinking of an episode of the 1990s CBS series *Northern Exposure*, which chronicled the travails of a young doctor working off his medical school debts in a small Alaskan town. Remember Ed, the feckless young Inuit who spent all his time watching old movies? Remember how an arcane ceremony revealed that he was destined to be a shaman? But Ed had no grounding in the Native American myths and traditions that a true shaman needs to be successful, and he felt completely in over his head. But then he realized: movies had already taught him everything he needed to know to assist his spiritual charges. With *A TV Guide to Life*, I propose to be the reader's shaman. And the fact that I just told that story about Ed from *Northern Exposure* from memory without having to look up a single one of the particulars is a powerful indication that I'm qualified to do so.

People say that the best way to learn is by doing. This is, of course, crap. But at the same time, keep in mind that there's only so much you can learn—really understand and internalize—just by sitting on your tuchas in front of the tube. Naturally you realize that already, or you wouldn't have bought this book to supplement your knowledge. I look forward to receiving letters from readers just like you (or their next of kin) telling me how these real-world applications of TV-gained knowledge went, and accept no legal or criminal liability for anything that may befall you or them as a result.

So here goes. Don't touch that dial. Because if your TV is old enough to still have a dial to begin with, it's likely to break off in your hand.

1

Saved by the Bell

School on TV

Nearly everyone has gone to school, and it's possible to learn almost as much there as it is from TV. So TV schools must be doubly educational, right? Just think about that time on *The Wonder Years* when Kevin had to drive his teacher to the hospital while she was in labor. I don't care how much homework *your* teacher gives you; she's never going to match an educational experience like that.

ELEMENTARY

We should begin at the beginning. But to do that, we have to go pretty far back. Back before TV, in fact, to the nineteenth-century one-room schoolhouse on

Little House on the Prairie. Before I started grade school, that's what I expected school to be like, only with fewer overalls and a smaller proportion of kids with feathered hair. So naturally, I was quite surprised when I arrived for my first day of kindergarten and didn't see my older sister—then in third grade and thus at the far end of a two-block-long building—the whole day.

Despite my initial confusion, I've since decided that the current system works better. Teaching toddlers and teenagers the alphabet and algebra all at the same time doesn't exactly sound like a recipe for no child left behind. Plus, the modern equivalent of a Willie Oleson can only ever disrupt one classroom in one grade at a time, as opposed to the entire school district like the original could. He always seemed to be in *my* classroom and *my* grade, but I'm sure the seven hundred other kids in my elementary school appreciated my sacrifice.

Obviously, I was quick to learn that grade school was different than it was on TV. Any illusions I might have had to the contrary were shattered the first time I was called on and stood up from my desk to talk. I thought that was what you were supposed to do, because that's how everyone did it on TV. Then sometime in sixth grade I finally figured out what all the other kids were snickering about and I quit it.

HIGH SCHOOL

But I had no reason to suspect that high school was so different as well. Why wouldn't it be a place of unfettered freedom, where the students were also adults and the teachers were all wise and inspiring (except the stupid ones, who were only ever around for a week before the wise and inspiring ones smacked them down anyway)?

And yet I was surprised nonetheless. The first surprise was when all the teachers failed to call me "Mr. Alexander." On rare occasions when a teacher did call one of my classmates "Mr." or "Miss" something, it meant that classmate was in serious trouble.[1]

Also, high school on television clearly demonstrates that every regular speaking cast member will not only have every class together, they will also sit next to one another, regardless of which letter their last names begin with.[2] This helps with the whispering among classmates during a teacher's lecture. On TV even the classes in overcrowded, inner-city schools filled with "at-risk," "underprivileged" teens like those on *Boston Public* never seem to have more than twenty or so kids in them. This is probably to save costs on extras, and also to facilitate said sitting together and whispering—whispering that somehow escapes the teacher's notice for minutes at a time yet is loud enough to almost completely drown out the teacher's words during the duration of the clandestine conversation. But beware, because after a few moments the teacher will either bust you, call on you unsolicited, or summon you up to the blackboard to provide a demonstration of the concept to which you haven't been paying a lick of attention (which is bad enough in a math class, but excruciating in health, especially during the sex-ed unit).

Whispering isn't the only way to communicate in secret during class, but it's certainly the safest. I don't say it's the most reli-

---

1. Naturally this never ever happened to me.

2. Oddly enough, my high school classes were filled with *completely different* students every period. Weird.

able, because that honor belongs to passing notes in class. Pass a note, and you *will* get pinched—rely on that.

This is something that everyone—not just me—learned from TV. The consequences are simply not worth it. Because as everyone knows, if the teacher catches you, then you have to come to the front of the class and read the note out loud (or, worse, your teachers will read it to the class, and with a great deal more gusto than they use to present the class materials). The contents of these notes are invariably humiliating; otherwise they wouldn't be in a note in the first place. We've all witnessed scenes on the small screen wherein a secret dalliance or crush is exposed before a roomful of snickering teenagers. It's an atavistic nightmare, comparable to showing up in your underwear for a final exam you didn't know about while a masked serial killer stalks the hallways, which, by the way, are on fire. No matter what you wrote, its very presence in a secret note renders the most innocuous sentiments utterly mortifying. If you're still in high school, try this experiment: get caught passing a note that reads, "Mr./Ms.——is a fantastic teacher, and has certainly brought out the best in what was already a marvelous group of students. I'm proud to be present for something so very special." No? Didn't think so.

CHANGING TIMES

The other thing about high school is that it's a lot harder to get through now than it used to be. Back in the fifties, the first golden age of TV, the problems that most concerned teachers were things like "students chewing gum" and "too much talking in the halls." Now they're things like "stab wound between third and fourth rib" and "three bullets in the temporal lobe." It ain't like it used to be.

And the TV of the times reflects this. On *The Many Loves of Dobie Gillis*, the biggest problem Dobie ever faced was how to land a date. Now, in his case, this was certainly a challenge not to be underestimated, since one of his classmates was played by a startlingly young Warren Beatty. It's hard enough for an average-looking guy like Dobie to get any action as it is, without that dude salting your game decades before Annette Bening turns up.

But then *Dobie Gillis* wasn't a true representation of high school any more than any other TV of that time was a true representation of anything else. For that, you have to fast-forward to the seventies. The inner city, even. Where, instead of classes with a dozen people presided over by a teacher in a suit and tie, we saw, well, classes with a dozen other people presided over by a different teacher in a suit and tie. The main difference between *Dobie Gillis* and, say, *Welcome Back, Kotter* was that the classroom on the latter show was a little more run-down-looking, and the suited teacher sported a white man's Afro and a Freddie Mercury mustache. Other than that, the students were pretty much equally dangerous.

THE COOL KIDS

Welcome Back, Kotter was a huge hit, and notable for its pioneering of the "let's give an obscure stand-up comedian his own sitcom" school of show development. It was supposed to be set in the mean streets of New York, in a tough school populated by a multiculti group of hoods called "sweathogs." These four guys epitomized 1975 cool (if that isn't an oxymoron). Well, at least three of them did. Freddie Washington, Juan Epstein, and Vinnie Barbarino seemed kind of edgy and dangerous (despite the latter's questionable decision to merge his name with a Beach Boys tune about a girl to create his own theme song, combined with his insistence on singing it at every possible opportunity). Adenoidal nerd Arnold Horshack was somebody they would have typically knifed and hung from the school flagpole within five minutes of meeting him, yet he too got to be part of the inner circle. Does this mean that *Kotter* dates back to before the invention of cliques?

Probably not, actually, because the concept of the high school clique on TV still kind of needed some dents hammered out decades later. Look no further than Bayside High School, where all of the smart, popular, good-looking kids hang out with each other—and an incredibly grating nerd named Samuel Powers, aka Screech.

I hope I'm not the first to ask why the best-dressed, best-looking (at least by early nineties standards) kids at the California high school that was the setting for *Saved by the Bell* put up with that Screech kid at all. I also freely admit that I haven't seen every episode, so maybe I just missed the one where we learned that he had photos of Zack and Slater together, taken at sleepaway camp years before, when the two ever-horny youths were in an experimental mood. It certainly wasn't because Screech was the brains of any given week's particular operation; how many of Zack's carefully laid plans were undone after an indiscreet utterance by Screech, inevitably punctuated by a high-pitched

"Oops!" I always thought Zack's life would have gone a lot more smoothly if he just refrained from telling Screech his plans, or indeed anything at all, including "hello."

The bond between Zack and Screech must have been a powerful one, because Zack even ended up dragging Screech to the same university with him in *Saved by the Bell: The College Years*. Maybe it was some kind of mutual wingman thing motivating Zack to assist Screech in his endless pursuit of Lisa, in return for Screech always derailing Zack's latest Kelly-related scheme. But even that doesn't hold up, because for a while there Screech dated a character played by Tori Spelling, which is, of course, the last time I believed any television character was actually attracted to any other television character who was played by Tori Spelling (including the guy who played her husband on her reality show).

Which conveniently brings us to another California high school, in the zip code 90210. Despite what we've just learned in the preceding paragraphs, everyone talks about the cliquishness of high school, and how hard it is to get in with the cool kids. And yet a couple of earnest, self-serious dorks from Minnesota named Walsh somehow became the center of the social scene at West Beverly Hills High on *Beverly Hills 90210*. Clearly something is amiss here. They obviously knew something I didn't, because I'm pretty sure that if I had moved from my Minnesota home to the richest high school in the country at that age and tried hanging out with the popular kids, I'd still be picking cotton threads out of my butt twenty years later.

And it wasn't just the Minnesota kids who got to hang either. Newspaper geek Andrea got to be part of the gang, despite looking like everyone's mom (or perhaps because of it). And drip-hop wannabe David scored a relationship with hideous-but-rich virgin Donna despite being a total loser (although not, I hasten to add, *quite* enough of a loser to be credibly attracted to Tori Spelling). And of the original cast, that pretty much leaves balding, bemulleted horndog Steve; insipid glamour-puss Kelly; and daddy-issued Dylan . . . actually, now that I think of it, both Screech and *90210* show us that getting in with the "cool kids" is not only easier than I thought for would-be social outcasts; it's overrated. Go for it, you guys, but try not to be too disappointed when you get there.

Actually, the most credible early warning I had about what high school would really be like was *Square Pegs*. Lead characters Lauren and Patty thought they had a foolproof plan for becoming popular, just by always being in the faces of the popular kids. The hell of it was that since only about half a dozen students in their entire high school actually had speaking parts, some form of interaction was in fact inevitable. I just wish I'd known at the time that status in high school doesn't necessarily translate to the same status in adulthood. For instance, nerdy Patty Greene was played by Sarah Jessica Parker, who of course ended up as a cultural icon on *Sex and the City*. Whereas Jami Gertz, who played rich preppy Muffy Tepperman, wound up in a considerably lower-class role on *Still Standing*, in one of many hot-chick/fat-guy sitcom iterations.[3] And the chick who played Jennifer De-Nuccio, the pinnacle of popularity at Weemawee High School? Her highest-profile gig after that was playing the nun sidekick to Howard Cunningham from *Happy Days* on the *Father Dowling Mysteries*. And as a character with a guy's name, no less. I

---

3. See chapter 3, "Tell Me Why I Love You Like I Do."

wouldn't wish that fate on the snottiest, most stuck-up girl in my class, even if I could remember who she was.

If you're über-popular in high school, perhaps the best thing you can do to ensure that your life hasn't already peaked is to arrange some kind of status-destroying humiliation for yourself in front of the entire student body. Better to endure one of your own choosing now than to be dealt one by destiny years down the road in some unknown fashion that you can't control.

SO-CALLED HIGH SCHOOL

Although *Square Pegs* was considerably more realistic in some ways than other high-school-set shows that had come before it (and many that came after), it was still kind of idealized. All of the characters fitted neatly into specific types like some kind of proto–*Breakfast Club* social experiment. And then *My So-Called Life* premiered in 1994, serving as a much more accurate reflection of how messy high school really can be.

Like the episode where Brian asked Delia to the dance because he knew she liked him, but then Angela asked Brian, so Brian canceled with Delia because he liked Angela, but Angela was only asking Brian so she could see Jordan there. And then the guy Rickie was after turned out to be straight, so that was a whole separate hairball. This is what I remember most about high school—lots of people liked lots of other people, but nobody ever seemed to really like the people who liked them. But what about all the people who paired off, you ask, and ended up as couples for months at a time and sometimes even years, if not the rest of their lives? Well, they liked each other least of all.

High schools are, ultimately, a messy stew of hearts and hormones all swirling around together in the smallest possible space. Don't feel bad about not having gotten out of there with your dignity intact, because nobody did. Even dreamy Jordan Catalano will always have to live with the embarrassment of having mistakenly addressed Brian as "Brain."

Angela nailed it in the pilot when she quit the yearbook staff. As she told her faculty adviser, "If you made a book of what *really* happened, it would be a really upsetting book." No shit. The best advice anyone can carry away from *My So-Called Life* is to have a friend like Rayanne. High school is a nightmare no matter what, and it will help to have a close friend who's more screwed up than you are.

HALLS OF FEAR

Still, things didn't get really scary until a few years later on in the nineties. I'm thinking about a show that, in a very real sense, owes its existence to the movie *Scream*, a clever, self-referential horror film that messed with viewers' expectations by not only defying cliché, but also by playing with the conventions of the genre. Sounds like *Buffy the Vampire Slayer*, right? Actually I'm talking about *Dawson's Creek*, which was created by *Scream* writer Kevin Williamson.

I'm actually glad *Creek* didn't start until I was well out of high school. If I had seen it before starting ninth grade, I would have completely stressed myself out thinking that once I graduated junior high, I would be expected to start talking in long, complete sentences about my feelings. How these kids could all spout off like they were in an advanced stage of therapy is completely beyond me. Not to mention how disappointed I would have been if I had arrived at my first day of high school and discovered that girls who look like Katie Holmes are not in fact the plain ones.

But let's get back to Buffy Summers, who hit Sunnydale High School at about the same time. *Buffy* was often an allegory of how dangerous high school really is, on a literal level.[4] You had a protagonist who had to deal with the fact that her first sexual partner went totally evil as soon as they'd done it, authority figures who couldn't be trusted, and parent-teacher conferences. It's enough to give anyone the screaming heebie-jeebies even now. Even leaving aside the fact that the very mention of the word *allegory* continues to trigger nervous flashbacks about English paper assignments that were way over my head.

Even so, apparently the whole *Buffy* experience was too fantasy-scary for some people, because they were looking for something a little less fluffy, like *Veronica Mars*. In the pilot, we learned that Veronica had not only fallen from grace as a popular kid at a rich school and been dumped by her wealthy, perfect boyfriend (okay, allegedly perfect; Duncan always struck me as a total dud), but also that her best friend had been murdered and Veronica herself had been roofied and raped at a party. By the time the season was over, we also learned that mother was

---

4. In fact, there were a couple of occasions when Buffy got too real. In 1999, the year of the Columbine High School shootings, the WB network pulled the airing of an episode called "Earshot" that was supposedly about a plot to commit a school shooting. Of course, *Buffy* being *Buffy*, the expected shooting rampage turned out to be nothing but a bullet-riddled red herring to divert attention from a cafeteria worker's rat-poison plot and another student's planned suicide attempt (with a sniper rifle in the clock tower, but then Jonathan, the would-be suicide, always was a little weird). Still, it was judged to be too close to home.

an alcoholic who had abandoned her family; that Veronica's ex-boyfriend might actually be her brother;[5] and that her friend's murderer was the father of ex-enemy, now-boyfriend. We're supposed to think that all of this made Veronica tough, and I have no problem believing this at all. She must have been, because after going through that litany of horrifying experiences, it's amazing that she didn't turn into a walking strip of jerky. We're always being told that children must be protected, sheltered, kept safe from the real world. Which is clearly nonsense. *Veronica Mars* shows us that the minority of people who say that young people can be surprisingly resilient don't go far enough; clearly, if Veronica is representative of the demographic, they're practically bulletproof.

Given all of the above, I was very glad to be out of high school by the time those shows were on. In fact, at this point I'm seriously considering homeschooling my own son. Not for the usual reasons of public schools being inadequate for modern educational needs and/or hotbeds of secular humanism, but primarily so he doesn't end up on drugs or get eaten.

FAILED TO MEET EXPECTATIONS

TV also encouraged me to believe that any group of high school students in possession of musical instruments could instantly become a band and perform polished musical numbers in the

---

5. We discovered in the second season that Veronica had also been raped by another perp that same night, who later turned out to be a killer who had given her chlamydia in the process. Perhaps it's actually best for all concerned that *Veronica Mars* was canceled after the third season, before we could discover any more trauma for Veronica.

cafeteria, just like on *Fame*. I suffered through three years of junior high school band in preparation for the very day when my similarly musically inclined peers and I would suddenly develop the ability to read one another's minds the way those kids at the School of the Arts always seemed to be able to, spontaneously tossing off songs as though they'd been rehearsing them for weeks. But then I discovered that whatever gland is supposed to make that possible doesn't actually develop or become active at age sixteen, as I had previously assumed. Not even taking up the electric guitar worked, for me or for anyone else.

Oh, and also? They didn't allow musical instruments in my cafeteria.

And the fact that all the students on TV are milling around in the hallways talking, and don't start heading to class until *after* the bell rings? That took me a while to get used to as well. People would start to head off to their rooms and I'd be like, "Where's everyone going? The bell doesn't ring for another thirty seconds, people."

THE COLLEGE YEARS

Graduation is a bittersweet time, because you've been with these people for years, living together through some of the most intense experiences of your young lives. But don't worry, because when it's over, if teenagers in real life are anything like teenagers on TV, you're all going to go to the same college together after you graduate.

Despite ninety percent of the people on TV living in either New York or California, where there are hundreds of colleges and universities, they always seem to end up at the one tiny (i.e., fictional) college closest to home. Buffy and Willow and Oz all ended up at UC-Sunnydale, and while Xander never actually enrolled, he always seemed to be on campus anyway. And Cordelia probably would have landed there too if she hadn't decided to walk off Sunnydale High's charred commencement grounds and then go straight to L.A. and right into her midthirties.

Everyone on *Veronica Mars* went to Hearst College in season three—even Wallace, who was supposedly a basketball phenom who could have written his own ticket in the NCAA despite being five and a half feet tall. And I don't remember the name of the schools where the *Beverly Hills 90210* folks matriculated, or where two-thirds of the *Saved by the Bell* cast spent :*The College Years,* but it's not like they had to keep in touch via Facebook either. Even Rory Gilmore and Paris Geller, who initially hated each other on *Gilmore Girls,* ended up as roommates at Yale University.[6]

It even works retroactively. We had just met Felicity from *Felicity* when she spent her pilot episode deciding to latch on to some guy from her high school and follow him across the country to the University of New York. This despite the fact that he didn't even know who she was at the time. Everyone else on the show questioned her seemingly impetuous decision, but the truth is that once a window of prime time opened up on her life, she had no choice. She was just lucky that Ben went to a school in a real city instead of doing what most TV characters do and heading off to some jerkwater diploma mill like UC-Faketown.

But the point is, now we're in college, where everyone in

---

6. I admit that I didn't follow the show in later years, so I suppose it's possible that, given the machine-gun dialogue on that show, they actually went to Yell University instead. I could be wrong.

the faculty finally does address the students by their last names, right? Wrong. The only time that ever happened to me was in my Japanese[7] classes, and even then I was "Alexander-san."

But there are other ways in which TV prepares you for college as well as it does for real life. For instance, you learn that professors having affairs with students is very, very bad, and also that it happens all the time. You learn that getting caught in the act of plagiarism or some other form of academic dishonesty is also very, very bad, and that it also happens all the time, and it will get your ass kicked right out of college unless you're a series lead. This last is a particularly dangerous lesson, because if everyone is the star of their own TV show in their heads, college students are even more so, and thus consider themselves able to get away with this kind of thing with impunity. How else to explain all the Web sites where you can buy a term paper? When tempted to fall into this trap, it's best to remind yourself that while you may well be the lead in your own series, you're only a secondary character in someone else's. In some, you're only recurring. And for everyone else, you're just an extra walking across the quad.

And don't tell me your college didn't have a quad. All colleges have quads.

But what happens after you graduate? Will you still continue to see all the same people? In most cases, no, because shows where the characters start in high school usually end before those same characters exit college. The aforementioned graduation of Rory and Paris just happened to coincide with the cancellation

---

7. It behooves me here to point out that I chose Japanese to fulfill my university's language requirement because I figured that after watching the miniseries *Shōgun* in its entirety, I had a good head start. Not even kidding here.

of *Gilmore Girls*, for example. Which is just as well. In those few cases where friends stick together all the way from sophomore year to the real world, nobody will admit to watching the post-college seasons. Remember how *Beverly Hills 90210* ended? Neither does anyone else.

CONCLUSION

And with graduation, we end this chapter. Of course lots of people continue their academic careers after the ceremony. But they're all in med school, and when they leave the campus and start going to the hospital instead, they're in the domain of chapter 6. Let's hope they have their lives a little more together by the time we catch up with them there.

Learning Experiences

1 Chart where all of your friends sit in relation to you in every class you have. Are you generally in the middle of the group? Somewhere on the edge? Does it vary by class or subject? If all of your friends are not in all of your classes, complain to your school system's superintendent.

2 In your entire graduating class, think of five or six people who would get lines every week in a TV series. Would you watch that show? If not, drop out and get a GED.

3 Get the cool kids at your high school to let you hang out with them. If you've already graduated, no fair offering to buy them liquor.

4 Go to high school. Get a diploma. Graduate. If you have already done this, do it again. Knowing now what you didn't know then, this time you will get much better grades and mad tail. If this is your first time, God help you.

5 Take a survey of a group of high school seniors to find out where they're going to college. Make sure you ask them in the form of a multiple-choice question, with only two or three options. At least one of these options should be fictional.

2

I'll Be There for You

Friends on TV

I have an idea for a TV show. It's about a group of friends who live together, work together, and play together, and they never fight or disagree because they all share the same values, priorities, and goals (although not in a mutually exclusive way). I call it *Test Pattern*. I think the relationship between Magenta and Black will be particularly vibrant.

Yes, obviously we all know that drama is conflict, and conflict is drama, and without both you can't have comedy either. Just colors on a screen. But there's more to it than that. There must be, or there wouldn't be so many famous groups of TV friends that make no sense whatsoever.

ENDURANCE

As we learned in the previous chapter, high school friendships may last for years, no matter how nonviable they may seem to the outside observer. There may be a simple explanation for this: sometimes it's just too much of a pain to shake off a friend that you're still going to see all the time because you spend every single day sitting right next to them, and if you're not talking anymore, who are you going to whisper to in class? But that doesn't explain why free, reasonable, emancipated adults choose to continue hanging around friends who are just as incompatible as the ones they were thrown together with by the public education system.

Ever try to schedule a lunch date with someone in New York? Just one other person who lives and works there? It's a nightmare. Add two other people with their equally busy schedules, and it becomes an exponentially greater logistical challenge, on par with a moon landing. And yet the women of *Sex and the City* managed it with astonishing regularity. Let's ignore for a moment the fact that they seemed to lunch at a different place every time, never had to make any panicked cell phone calls all *"Where is this place again?,"* and almost always seemed to manage a full quorum (and when they didn't, it was a big fucking deal). Not to mention, I can't figure out how "traditional" (read: uptight and judgmental) Charlotte could be in the same room with man-hungry she-bachelor (read: fictional) Samantha for more than five minutes without one of them twisting the other's head off. Miranda seems like the only one with half a brain in her head, so it's a mystery as to how she can stand either one of them. Let alone Carrie, whose chronic "but enough about me—let's talk about me" syndrome manages to be completely obnoxious yet not debilitating enough to prevent her from using her friends' deeply personal experiences as fodder for her columns. The only way they could possibly stay friends in the face of Carrie's regular and syndicated violations of their confidence is if they don't read her column at all. In which case, what kind of friends are they all in the first place?

This uncertain brand of friendship seems to be pandemic among New York–based foursomes. Think about the main cast of *Seinfeld*. You had Jerry, a self-absorbed stand-up comic who always talked like he was onstage; George, an even more self-absorbed schlub loser whose best quality was his less-than-dashing good looks; Kramer, a slightly less self-absorbed yet utterly exhausting specimen of a man with serious boundary issues; and Elaine, who made up for her few redeeming qualities by always dragging some insufferable significant other into the mix. How anybody could stand any of them is beyond me. As far as I'm concerned, the most popular guy on the show should have been Newman.

Of course you can't have a chapter about friends without talking about *Friends*. But to be honest, I don't remember much about it. I wasn't a regular viewer. I found it cloying and contrived, and it wasn't my idea of a good time to watch a group of eleven-year-olds exchange alleged cute-icisims during the ABC family hour. Even way back in 1979. The NBC sitcom of the same name that premiered in 1994 was much better, I thought.

The amazing thing about *Friends* (version 2.0) wasn't that it lasted for ten years; the amazing thing was that the friendships depicted thereon lasted even longer. But then *Friends* was always careful to keep the interrelationships overlapping, if only to make otherwise inevitable breakups all but logistically impossible. For instance, Joey and Chandler hung out all the time because they were roommates,[1] and they also hung out with Monica and Rachel because they lived across the hall, and then Ross hung out with them because Monica was his sister and he and Chandler had been best friends since college and Ross didn't have anyone else to hang out with, and then Phoebe . . . wait, I'll get back to you on Phoebe.

Later in the run, the group dynamic changed. Monica and Chandler fell in love, moved in together, and got married, while Rachel got pregnant and spent, like, a whole season waffling between Joey and Ross, eventually ending up back with Ross, while Phoebe . . . damn, here we are again.

Even the show seemed to be aware of Phoebe's precarious status in the tribe. At one point, Rachel remarked that she always thought the first to fall by the wayside would be Phoebe. Alluding to a few of the points I made above, she explained, "You lift right out."[2]

But the worst friend I can think of—not just on TV, but in the entire world, in all of history—was on *Will & Grace*. No, I'm not talking about either of the two title characters; although

---

1. Except for a brief period when Joey moved out and Crazy Eddie moved in, which taught us the valuable lesson that people we don't already know are completely bugfuck.

2. It wasn't just that. It was also that Phoebe was a pain in the ass. Barely more functional than her twin sister, Ursula (whose existence allows me to annoy people with my theory that *Friends* is nothing more than a *Mad About You* spin-off), Phoebe was always dragging everyone down with her flakiness and irresponsibility. From the time she sat on hold on Monica's phone for two days with Utah, to just about every time she opened her mouth to say something cluelessly unsupportive, they really would have been better off without her. Plus her brother was creepy. So why did she get to hang around? Well, Phoebe's occupation was massage therapist, so maybe she spent a lot of offscreen time giving the boys happy endings.

they were both black holes of emotional neediness, at least they usually took turns being wrecks for each other. And although Karen had her faults (self-absorption, elitism, a voice that only dogs could hear), she also had the powerfully redeeming characteristic of being fabulously rich. No, when I refer to the worst friend ever, I'm of course talking about Jack McFarland. "Just Jack," as he styled himself, although there was nothing just about him.

Jack was, to put it bluntly, an asshole. Unabashedly and spectacularly self-absorbed, he contributed nothing positive to the dynamic. All of us have good and bad qualities, and so do our friends. They balance out in different ways. It's what makes us unique. But Jack was nothing but pages and pages of ledger paper covered in red ink. His best quality was that he lacked the ambition or seriousness of purpose to enter politics, which almost certainly saved untold numbers of lives.

I'm not saying that Jack wasn't an entertaining character, or that the show wouldn't have been greatly diminished without him. His presence was certainly a boon for the audience. But he was the kind of "friend" that people write to advice columns about:

Dear Syndicated Advice Columnist,

I have this friend. Only I'm not sure I should call him that anymore. I always thought friends are supposed to be supportive and be there for each other. But this friend (let's call him "Jack") treats friendship like a one-way street—going his way. He's always "borrowing" money I never see again, and my unflagging support of his dead-end career never seems to be reciprocated. He does have a sense of humor, but his jokes are always mean-

spirited and usually about my ass. Should I feel guilty for thinking
I deserve better?
A Bad Friend?

One hopes that the advice columnist would respond thusly:

Dear Friend,
Recommend that your friend meet with a reputable therapist.
When he arrives at the appointment, jump out from the bushes
and shoot him in the face.

Actually, that advice columnist would say that when people treat us badly, it's because we let them. And why do we let them? Because they have a three-year, half-million-per-episode contract and there's nothing we can do about it.

It's easy for us to look at friendships like this and judge them from our removed, impartial vantage point. Just like it's easy to tell who's wrong in a dispute in which we aren't involved. We just can't always see the folly of our own position.

And plus, breaking up with a friend is always such a trial. There's always all manner of on-the-nose yelling and recriminations, and most of the time you just make up by the end of the episode anyway. You could just stop calling the other person, but then you'll inevitably end up accidentally and awkwardly running into them on the street. This is unavoidable even if you live in a city of nine million people, like the time *Sex and the City*'s Charlotte and Miranda were on the outs about the latter's plan to have an abortion while the former had been struggling to get pregnant. So of course they bumped into each other—by pure chance—as if there could be a single atom of what one might call "rendezvous-karma" left between them after all the lunches they were constantly managing to have together.

CONFLICT RESOLUTION

Conflict is drama, and drama is conflict. My original editor disagreed with that assessment, so I beat him up. You should have seen it. It was awesome.

It's true, though. There's a reason reality-show producers constantly cast people who pride themselves on not being able to get along with anyone: nobody's going to tune in for an hour of "after you, no, *please*, after *you*, no, I *insist*, after *you*." They tried it with a team on *The Amazing Race* one season, and the only reason the Cho brothers lasted more than a week was that other people were just naturally even slower. I'd go on about the kind of televised conflict that is carefully staged and planned out ahead of time in such a way that the producers know exactly what will transpire, but as I've said before, I'm trying to stay away from reality TV in this book.

Fortunately, there's a lot to learn from scripted television about conflict resolution. Especially in the case of shows that center around groups of friends who aren't forced to stay together by familial relationships, a shared workplace, or other external factors. If all these folks can continue to hang with one another for years despite disagreeing all the time, they really must be onto something when it comes to getting past even the most hostile disagreements. Fortunately for you (and my friends), I've figured out what it is. The rules are simple.

1 Keep the discussion limited to the issues at hand. Dragging in stuff that didn't happen within the last half hour or hour does nobody any good. You can't be sure that everyone even saw that episode.

2 You may be tempted to say something funny. Go ahead. Even if your antagonist doesn't laugh, somebody somewhere will.

3 After five minutes, wrap it up. Don't forget the appropriate sign of affection.

And that's it. The problem is, the person you're in conflict with may not have seen the same shows you and I have, and therefore may not be aware of the rules. Pointing out these rules will, experience has taught me, only make them madder.

We all tend to view our personal conflicts from our own selfish perspectives. But when we see other friends, coworkers, spouses, and family members working out their differences while safely separated from them by a TV screen, we get to enjoy a more impartial perspective. We can look at things from both sides. And perhaps from that, we can take away the lesson that when conflict arises in our own lives, it's not just because the other person is being a selfish ass. It's because we probably are, too.

It's going to take some practice before you can get good at these techniques, so before you try any of them out on your friends, practice with family members and other people who are stuck with you no matter what. You'll quickly realize that seeing things from the other person's perspective is, bar none, the fastest way to resolve a conflict. It's also really hard. It's even harder to do it quickly, and hardest of all when the person in question is yelling at you. But practice makes perfect, so it's probably a good idea to keep watching reruns of *Everybody Loves Raymond* and *The King of Queens* until you get the hang of how it's done. And if your significant other complains about how much time you're spending on this project, just tell them to stuff it.

Once you've learned all there is to learn about conflict resolution from TV, all your problems can be resolved in thirty minutes or an hour. We saw this all the time, for example, on *Family Ties*. One of the Keatons would do something stupid or selfish (it was usually Alex), hilarity would ensue, and then Steven and/or Elyse would blow another inch of dust off their entropying authority over the household, triggering a confrontation. It helps if all your confrontations are, like theirs, miniature transactional analysis workshops with everyone always effortlessly using their "I feel" statements and trying to understand one another's point of view. Otherwise, every argument would have ended with somebody spitting, "Screw you, Alex!" and then grabbing him by his tie and punching him in the head. At first glance, the televised version seems preferable. However, moderation in all things is advised; keep in mind that if Alex had lived with a normal family instead of a bunch of doormats, maybe he would have moved out before he turned thirty-five.

Your life will also be a lot easier if you learn to argue like they do on TV. Arguments in real life aren't nearly as much fun, anyway. No one ever says what they really mean; they either hold back to avoid saying something they'll regret later, or they go right ahead and cross that same line, and then the argument becomes about that instead of what it was originally about. Scripted arguments are much more satisfying. And when someone on TV gets in a really good zinger, the scene cuts to someone else or goes to commercial. This may take some practice in real life. I've tried it. The best you can hope for in your first attempt is an indignant, "Hey, come back here, we're talking!" Or possibly getting grabbed by the tie and punched in the head.

BIRDS OF A FEATHER. NOT.

See, part of the reason there's so much conflict on TV is that characters on the same show tend to be as different from one another as possible. Look around at your friends. Do you have anything in common with them? If so, you probably want to get new ones. You need several different types of characters for different segments of the population to relate to. For instance, *Seinfeld* could have been about four fussy, sarcastic, single guys in Manhattan, but that would have left the nation's high-haired, clownishly dressed, goofily entering demographic unrepresented, so they came up with Kramer. Underachieving, average-looking guys needed a relatable-to George Costanza character too. And of course Elaine was added to the mix for guys who like to look at attractive women.

There's a great deal to be learned from the reliable "fish out of water" scenario as well. If everyone on the show has the same background, there are many fewer opportunities for them to learn from one another, and to educate us in the process. For instance, while HBO's *Rome* effectively demonstrated how quickly history used to happen in the days before pants, it also missed a lot of opportunities. It could have been a much more instructional series, if not for the fact that everyone on the show was from the same culture. Because of that, none of the characters ever had to have any of those weird rituals or social rules explained to them for the benefit of us, the audience. What *Rome* really needed was an additional character, an accidental time traveler from twenty-first-century Indiana, to ask all the questions we viewers were wondering about all the time. Like, for instance, why everyone spoke with an English accent centuries before the invention of England, and could everyone please just stop having sex for ten minutes in a row.

Whereas one of the most educational shows ever was *The Beverly Hillbillies*. Name another show that more effectively delineated the differences between what some politicians have called "the two Americas" simply by making them bump into each other a lot. In their new lives, the Clampetts were asked to forget everything they knew and start learning a whole new set of social norms and conventions. If the Clampetts had owned a TV before striking it rich, none of the crazy stuff they encountered out west would have come as a surprise to them,[3] and you and I wouldn't have learned a thing.

Same goes for when African-American kids from the streets end up in cushy surroundings with rich new guardians. Okay, yes, Arnold Jackson on *Diff'rent Strokes* with his side-parted Afro was about as "street" as Tweety Bird, but Gary Coleman and Todd Bridges more than made up for their lack of thug cred later in life (to say nothing of Dana Plato). And yes, dropping a young black rapper into the Banks house on *Fresh Prince of Bel Air* was plenty scary for a comedy, but come on, it was Will Smith. If they really wanted to shake things up, they would have cast Ice-T during his "Cop Killer" era. Every family dinner would've car-

---

3. Oh, who am I kidding? Every time I stumble on some West Coast–based reality show like *The Real Desperate Housewives of the Laguna Beach Hills Go to Dr. 90210*, I'm completely flummoxed.

ried the very real risk of somebody getting shot. Which would have also been an advantage to the show's producers when it came time to negotiate the actors' contracts.

But you don't have to be from a totally different walk of life to sometimes have trouble seeing where your friends are coming from. Even a couple of folks from a seemingly homogenous sub-culture like, say, the FBI, might work together to find enough un-common ground to disagree all the time. Part of what made *The X-Files* work as long as it did was the fact that it revolved around the relationship between a skeptic and a believer. In a weird way, having them argue about vampires and aliens and what not actu-ally made the far-fetched goings on around them seem more plau-sible. The show didn't expect you to just swallow everything; it made it so Mulder was always having to defend his far-out theories to Scully, and, by extension, to us. The show would have been a dismal failure with two believers. Make a show about *three* believ-ers, and you get something even worse: *The Lone Gunmen.*[4]

On the other hand, it's much better to avoid conflict than to constantly give in to it. Aren't the best, most "quality" shows about long-term angst and festering resentment, while the shows where everyone argues all the time seem kind of tacky? And which kind of show would you rather be in?

DRAMATIC ACCENTS

Have you heard that people who spend a lot of time together be-come more and more alike? They even begin to talk alike, shar-

---

4. See chapter 13, "A Different World Than Where You Come From," for more on *The Lone Gunmen* and other spin-offs.

ing the same speech cadences and expressions and diction that, over time, becomes its own shorthand. This is very well known. It's also nonsense.

That's because lots of peer groups have at least one person who stands out by speaking with an accent. This can work for you too. The faker and more exotic the voice, the better. Ideally, it should be totally invented. Genuine Asian, Jewish, African-American, Latino, or even Southern American speech patterns may do in a pinch, provided your fish-out-of-water surroundings are sufficiently uptight and otherwise linguistically homogeneous. And even if they're not, you can still stand out. There's a reason everyone in school wants to talk to the kid from Bolivia—he's the only person anyone knows who talks like that. Or at least he is until everybody else starts imitating him because he's so popular.

As with life, a lot of TV is all about being funny. A lot of TV is also all about talking. So if you can talk funny, you're golden. Or, alternatively, you're Bronson Pinchot. One of the two.

Not that being Bronson Pinchot in the eighties was such a rough gig. Back then you could still put on a whole show about a guy who talked funny—in this case, *Perfect Strangers*. This show also followed the *Odd Couple* principle of having different types of characters thrown together, because a guy talking funny around a bunch of other people talking funny stops being funny and starts getting boring in a hurry.[5] It's the clash of cultures and styles that keeps things interesting. Well, that and getting a couch stuck in an elevator.

---

5. For an extreme example of this, please refer to *The Star Wars Holiday Special*, which, among its many other capital crimes against art, included a lengthy scene of nothing but Chewbacca's family at home, growling and howling senselessly at one another for something like twenty minutes. A little Wookiee-ese, it turns out, goes a long way. A lot of it will damn near kill you.

We learned from *Perfect Strangers* that if you're only foreign enough, like Balki, you can get away with spewing a steady stream of malaprops and never have to manage a single English idiom, for as long as seven seasons. Yet if you have a cynical American cousin, your good nature and naïveté can teach him all sorts of valuable life lessons. But was that all Balki had to teach us? I always wondered if anybody ever used episodes of *Perfect Strangers* to try to learn Balki's native language, not knowing that the Myposian tongue was completely made up. Besides me, I mean.[6]

Moving forward in time (and also backward), there's Fez from the 1998–2006 series *That '70s Show*. That unlikely group of friends included a nerd with an out-of-his-league girlfriend, a pothead whose brother was in military school on *Malcolm in the Middle*, a shallow ditz, and Demi Moore's husband, so Fez had his work cut out for him in trying to stand out. Fortunately, he wasn't above pronouncing everything he said like a harelipped Latin American who learned English by teaching French as a second language to deaf Inuits. Nobody even knew what country Fez was originally from, let alone the origin of his accent. There was one episode in which he was supposedly about to be deported back home after vandalizing a water tower, but he got to stay in the United States. Reasons were given, yet I continue to suspect that it was only because the INS couldn't figure out where to send him back to.

There's really no downside. Even if you're a nonnative speaker and you occasionally have no choice but to fill in a lin-

---

6. One other useful thing I did learn from an episode of *Perfect Strangers* is that if you jump into a taxi and yell, "Follow that car," they won't. As a result, I have never once attempted it.

guistic gap with a phrase from your mother tongue, it's a sure thing that most of your English-speaking cohorts will understand that phrase anyway. And you can't get more convenient than that. For instance, a native Spanish-speaking character might remark, "Hey, *qué pasa*? Are you *hombres* ready to *vamonos, sí* or *no*? I have to stop at the doctor's office to pick up *mi madre*'s electrocardiogram because they think she might be developing congestive *corazón* failure. Your insistence on behaving in such a dilatory fashion is a profound annoyance. *¡Andale!*"

Clearly, the so-called language barrier is more of a permeable membrane than a real barrier. It's kind of always been this way. Back in the actual seventies, *The Life and Times of Grizzly Adams* portrayed a close friendship between two leads who didn't even speak the same language. The titular protagonist, played by Dan Haggerty, only spoke English, while his best friend, a North American black bear named Ben, only spoke bear. Adams's second-best friend was a Native American named Nakuma who also only spoke *his* native language. Once Adams and Nakuma got past the point in their relationship where they were most likely to have killed each other (and didn't), they eventually learned to understand each other. But not by speaking each other's language. Instead, each would simply speak his own tongue, and the other would be able to understand. In Adams's case, he could not only understand, but also answer Nakuma's remarks in a way that allowed us, the audience, to figure out what Nakuma had said in the first place. Adams was clearly ahead of his time here, as most TV characters who have to convey to the audience both sides of a one-sided conversation are able to do so with the assistance of telephones. Which, as of Adams's time, hadn't been invented.

After a lull of a few decades in this trend, both *Lost* (2004) and *Heroes* (2006) premiered with regular characters who didn't speak English at all. On the former show, the surviving (?) passengers of Oceanic Flight 815 included a Korean couple, Jin and Sun, whose communication with their fellow castaways was fairly limited by the fact that they stuck to their native language. Later, it turned out the wife, Sun, had secretly learned English before boarding the fateful flight. Her reasons ostensibly had something to do with escaping her old life under the control of her Mob-connected father, but I suspect that the truth is that three or four episodes with two non-English-speaking characters were as many as the writers had in them.

But becoming friends with your fellow castaways can steepen the language learning curve, apparently. In the sixty or so days of on-the-island time that the castaways endured in *Lost*'s first three seasons, Jin picked up a surprising amount of English as well. My admittedly vague understanding (and I didn't learn this from TV, so its veracity is in question) is that English is one of the hardest languages to learn, especially if your native language is not also a European one. Fortunately, it seems to be a lot easier to learn if you live in the TV.[7]

It can even work if your best friend speaks the same foreign language as you, as long as he also knows English. The other character who has been a beneficiary of the kind of high-speed language-immersion education that only television can provide is Hiro Nakamura, the Japanese time-and-space traveler on *He-*

---

7. The irony is that although Jin's portrayer, Daniel Dae Kim, was born in South Korea, he was raised in the United States and speaks English as his first language. So presumably, South Korean audiences of *Lost* are hugely entertained by listening to Kim's American-accented Korean. Unless of course he's getting his vocals dubbed into Korean like everyone else's.

roes. Like Jin, Hiro has been picking up the lingua franca in the express lane, despite having his friend Ando along to translate.[8] Hiro's learning English quickly enough to make me wonder if he isn't spending his commercial breaks teleporting in and out of ESL classes.

A third example that comes to mind was also a character from an Asian country. On HBO's *Deadwood*, the character called Wu was a Chinese national whose English was limited to *Swedgin* (his pidginized pronunciation of his best friend Al Swearengen's name) and *cocksucker*. It must have been frustrating for Wu to be on a show with the baroque linguistic stylings for which *Deadwood* was famous, but not really be able to participate. He just had to make up for it with other assets: an uncanny ability for mime, and a yardful of pigs that ate human remains. With such resources at one's disposal, along with his aforementioned alliance with the most dangerous man in town, understanding the subtle nuances that differentiate *cocksucker* from *motherfucker* doesn't seem quite as important.

Perhaps thousands of years in the future, all known languages will have consolidated into one worldwide tongue spoken exactly the same way by everyone. Which will mean that if TV shows of that distant time want to lean on the conceit of having characters who talk different, they'll either have to be set in their distant past or they'll have to cast someone who was flash-frozen in the twenty-first century and thawed out millennia later for that very purpose.

I nominate Bronson Pinchot.

---

8. And yes, being able to teleport is all well and good, but if I'm in a country where I don't speak the language and I have someone with me who can get us checked in to a hotel? That's *my* superhero.

CONCLUSION

How many times have you heard someone wonder, "Why are they even friends? They have nothing in common." Asked and answered, as this chapter plainly demonstrates. Friends can be from different backgrounds, speak different languages, even be different species. There's no excuse to eliminate someone as a potential friend just because they might be different from you in some superficial way.

Unless it's Jack McFarland. In which case you should run away as fast as you can.

Learning Experiences

1 Think about your group of friends, and which one is the odd one out. If you can't think of any, this means *you* are the odd one out and they're all wondering why they put up with you. Pick a new group of friends, and be sure to include an odd one out this time.

2 Have lunch with a friend in New York City. You may think that arranging this will be easier if you actually have a friend in New York City, or one who is visiting New York City at the time you are there, or even if you yourself are in New York City at the time. Go ahead and see if that makes a difference.

3 Leave your home and walk around randomly until you accidentally run into one of your friends on the street. It should only be a matter of minutes, so resist the temptation to bring along bottled water, lunch, cash, or identifying documents in the event you forget where you live. You probably don't even need to wear comfortable shoes.

4 Break up with a friend. Do it the opposite of the way you see it on TV, resisting the urge to yell or cry. But don't worry about what happens now that you don't have that friend anymore, because according to TV you didn't actually break up in the first place without all that nonsense.

5 Think about the person in your life who is most different from yourself. Think about your last disagreement, and how much of it was a result of the two of you simply having different values and different priorities, and how much of it was you just being a jerk. Yeah, I thought so.

6 Cultivate a fake accent. British is probably easiest, and you can manage it by watching a lot of public television, BBC America, and *This Is Spinal Tap*. British is therefore disqualified.

3

Tell Me Why
I Love You Like I Do

TV Couples

Relationships are a lot of work. Whether it's
a new romance, a long-term relationship,
a marriage, or a breakup, romantic pairings aren't
something you can just coast through. They can be
exhausting and demanding. And the more important it is to you to have your relationship succeed,
the more devastated you'll be when it eventually
doesn't. Perhaps the wisest course of action would
be to go through your whole life alone and single,
if only that weren't worse. For both you *and* your
ratings.

IDEAL COUPLES—DOOMED!

Some people are just made for each other. As soon as you meet them, you know that they would be perfect together. Watching the unresolved sexual tension between couples like this provides such a frisson that you can't wait for them to realize what is happening between them and finally admit their feelings for each other. For this reason, it is imperative for them to remain apart forever at all costs.

You know what I'm talking about. TV history is littered with the corpses of shows like *Moonlighting*, which, just as the best example, was built completely on the unresolved sexual tension between David and Maddie. "Resolving" it was inevitable, but it was also the worst thing that could have possibly happened to the show. *Moonlighting* was always a little on the silly side, with stunt-cast cameos from then superstars like Whoopi Goldberg and Judd Nelson (and right there is one scary snapshot of eighties celebrity culture), but by the time Maddie and David's unborn fetus was being voiced by Bruce Willis, it was time for everyone to get out of the pool. Plus we ended up with about seven hundred *Look Who's Talking* movies as a toxic by-product, so there was really no upside.

Not that *Moonlighting* was the first coed private-eye show characterized by shameless flirting. Remington Steele of *Remington Steele* was obsessed with films from the golden age of Hollywood, and his relentless banter with his mentor/business partner, Laura Holt, reflected that. Steele sweet-talked like a Cary Grant character, and was just as sexless. Even so, somehow Steele and Laura eventually got married, or were supposed to, until NBC canceled the show, then un-canceled it when star Pierce Brosnan was tentatively cast as James Bond, whereupon Brosnan had to turn down the role of Bond until *GoldenEye* years later. *Remington Steele* limped along for one more season, and James Bond was played instead by Timothy Dalton (who got critically and popularly pilloried for his trouble) in two lackluster 007 films. In short, the consummation of Laura's relationship with Steele ended up being either a major setback or detrimental to *Remington Steele*, NBC, Pierce Brosnan, his costar Stephanie Zimbalist (never seen again), Timothy Dalton, the James Bond film franchise, and fans of all of the above. Really, it was a lose/lose/lose/lose/lose/lose/lose situation. It just goes to show that no matter how ideal a potential couple may seem, circumstances beyond their control—and plain old bad timing—always have the power to keep them apart. This is clearly for the best, as the alternative appears to be a cascading series of disasters for everyone who is even tangentially involved.

Another way to keep a long-term romance story going is for only half of the couple in question to know about it. For example, so much of what drove *Frasier* during the first several seasons was Niles's secret, unrequited crush on Daphne. It seemed they could never be together, because Daphne worked for Niles's dad and Niles was an effeminate man married to an invisible wife. But *Frasier* was on the air for nine years, and nine years is a long time to nurse a secret, unrequited crush (unless you're in high school, when nine years can pass by in the course of sixth-period math). Eventually Niles divorced Maris, and Daphne nearly married Niles's divorce attorney before learning about Niles's feelings for her and ending up with him instead. As with Ross and Rachel on *Friends*, a hidden crush culminated in the object of said crush accidentally learning about it and finding herself returning her admirer's feelings. Which serves as a clear demonstration that the best way to win the heart of your secret love is to have someone reveal the secret. Preferably in a way that's as embarrassing to you as possible.

But what happens when there are two people with secret mutual crushes on each other, as with Jim and Pam on NBC's *The Office*? This is a much more symmetrical yet much more cursed nonromance (or no-mance, as I'm tempted to call it). They love all the same things (pop culture, sarcasm, each other) and, perhaps more importantly, hate all the same things (their boss, their coworkers, each other's significant other). Yet for three seasons, things just didn't seem to work out for them. And at the beginning of the fourth season, viewers discovered that the one thing that would doom the Jim-and-Pam relationship forever had occurred: they were actually dating. And the first few episodes of that season were pretty shaky. Combined, these two factors pointed to an uncertain future. At this point, nobody knows what sort of obstacles will come between them next. Maybe an interdimensional rift, or some sort of fundamental human–alien incompatibility thing. Stuff like that seemed to work for John Crichton and Aeryn Sun on *Farscape* for quite a while.

Sometimes the irresistible force keeping the ideal couple apart is . . . nothing at all. Mulder and Scully didn't actively flirt all that much, but they had their own cult of "shippers."[1] *The X-Files* was the show that launched the whole idea of shippers

---

1. In case you're unfamiliar with the term *shippers*, it's a shortened form of "relationshippers," which refers to fans who desperately wish for two characters on a TV show to initiate a romantic relationship with each other. Some of the most fanatical shippers have no relationships of their own, which is what they would probably be better off concentrating on.

in the first place, in fact. Buried in their work, always draped in drab G-man attire, constantly consigned to decidedly unglamorous surroundings, and dealing with stuff that was, a lot of times, let's face it, pretty gross, Mulder and Scully nonetheless always had people on the other side of the screen pulling for them to get together.

Maybe this almost universal desire reflects an inner struggle between the dual nature of audience members. To a certain extent, most people have a skeptical side that is reluctant to buy into anything that's not supported by science (like Scully). But the same people also have a side that looks for wonder in the world, the magical and the unexplained—the part of us that says, to quote Mulder's iconic flying-saucer poster, "I want to believe." Mulder and Scully represented the dual nature with which so many of us constantly struggle. A union between the two—even as obliquely paralleled by two allegorical representations like Mulder and Scully—might well mean finding every answer, solving every mystery, for all of us, from whom exactly the Cigarette Smoking Man works for to the very meaning of life itself. *The X-Files* made us realize that in a sense, every relationship is a quest for completion, an attempt to appropriate the complementary attributes of a person who is both like and yet unlike oneself.

Or maybe it was just because both of them were so damn good-looking.

But *The X-Files* also taught us that the dangers of a workplace romance, however they might have manifested for Mulder and Scully, must be daunting enough to avoid at all costs. Even though they clearly cared about each other, their professionalism and the extent to which they each valued their working relationship prevented either of them from making a move. Or at least that's what we're supposed to think. I know people who maintain that they were screwing like serious-faced bunnies every time a camera wasn't pointed at them. I always thought those were the people who *really* want to believe.

But they turned out to be right. In the end, of course, we found out that Mulder was in fact the father of Scully's sort-of-messianic baby, and not just biologically. Sure, he wasn't around for a while after being abducted by aliens, but their ultimate reunion bespoke more than just a working relationship. Not that anyone was still watching at that point, which only proves the danger of the *Moonlighting* pitfall all over again.

AFTER THE BREAKUP

But getting together doesn't necessarily have to be the end. The story of an enduring love can continue indefinitely, as long as you break up as soon as possible.

That worked great for Dave and Lisa on *NewsRadio*. They fell into bed together relatively shortly after the former started at WNYX. No long-drawn-out courtship for these two. Instead, they spent most of the series' run not dancing around unresolved sexual tension, but dealing with all the other unresolved crap from their abortive relationship. In other words, just because you and your partner aren't together anymore, it doesn't necessarily mean that interesting and/or funny things have to stop happening to you.

But then, in that department, nothing can touch *Friends*. Ross had the relationship-defining "on a break" tryst with the copy girl that broke up Rachel and him almost for good (although not always very effectively, as the existence of their child demonstrates) and cast its shadow all the way into the series finale a gazillion years later. So it's clear that while a fear of the future can keep lovers apart, it doesn't have anything on stuff from the past.

Just ask Lorelai and Luke from *Gilmore Girls*. Really, the only thing they really had in common when they got together was that they both cared about Rory and about Luke's Diner. And I'm not sure Luke was even all that fond of the latter. Maybe the real question is how they managed to stay together so long in the first place. Naturally, *Gilmore Girls* ended with the two of them back together, which means they're stuck that way in the public imagination. For good.[2]

Same with Carrie Bradshaw and John Big or whatever his name was on *Sex and the City*. They were a fairly lopsided couple when they got together (and not just because when side by side they looked like a canary standing next to a barn), so centrifugal forces were bound to pull them apart. But then they were saved by the laws of series finales, which—just like with Ross and Rachel and Lorelai and Luke—threw them back together at the eleventh hour. And despite the fact that Chris Noth never appears on any of Sarah Jessica Parker's beauty product commercials and Sarah Jessica Parker never turns up on *Law & Order: Oh, It's Chris Noth This Week*, everyone remembers them as living happily ever after. At least until the movie comes out.

What all of these couples teach us is that if two people are meant to be together—which, in most cases, they are—all they

---

2. Good for us, that is. Not good for them, because you know that somewhere they're driving each other up a wall again as you read this.

really need to do in order to make that happen is hold out until the series finale.

Oddly enough, the opposite is true as well. Almost as powerful as the repulsive force pushing ideal couples apart like poles of a magnet is the attractive force drawing together couples who are totally wrong for each other. Witness Sam and Diane on *Cheers,* who were such a dysfunctional couple that Diane actually left the show for years, and didn't come back until that breakneck finale episode.[3]

So maybe that's the key. One-third of *happily ever after* is *after.* Nobody ever used the phrase *happily ever during.*

HAPPILY EVER DURING

This isn't to say that you can't learn about how to stay together from TV. You can. It's just that you have to already be together when the show starts.

Back in the early nineties, many viewers wondered what lovely, smart, vivacious Helen Hunt (remember, this was the early nineties) ever saw in the whiny, neurotic gasbag played by Paul Reiser on *Mad About You.* Despite the fact that Paul Buchman was supposedly a documentary filmmaker in the same class as Ken Burns, he was self-absorbed, endlessly impressed with his own cleverness, and unable to ever shut up. The fact that he was an early popularizer of the catchphrase *not so much* has yet to be assigned to the plus or minus column.

But now we know: Jamie Buchman could see into the fu-

---

3. "Breakneck" in the sense that you wanted to break Diane's.

ture, and knew that the millennium held nothing for hot sit-com wives but tubby, schlubby husbands. Compared to the male leads with attractive missuses on more recent shows like *King of Queens*, *According to Jim*, *Still Standing*, *The Drew Carey Show*, and *Grounded for Life*, Reiser was a freaking triath-lete. Meanwhile, over on the one-hour-drama beat, Dennis Franz was working his way inexorably up the *NYPD Blue* hot-ness ladder like some kind of romance-oriented version of Richard III. Jamie Buchman had to lock that shit down, and fast.

Is it really that easy for everymen to land an attractive spouse? Well, no. There's more to it for guys than cracking open another beer, canceling your subscription to *Men's Journal*, and sitting back to wait for some svelte honey to come along and clamp herself to your pendulous jowls. What's it going to take? Well, if you're in the market for a wife who looks like Courtney Thorne-Smith or Jami Gertz[4] or Leah Remini, here's a quick list of things you need to do:

1. Be funny. Chicks dig a sense of humor.
2. Don't be funny to her. No matter how clever or witty your wisecracks and rants and little "bits" might be, no matter how uproarious the disembodied laughter that fills your house, all you'll ever get from the missus as a reward for your little performances is a look of annoy-ance. Don't be discouraged. This just means you need to do it more.
3. Screw up a lot. Like, a lot. Forget about anniversa-

---

4. See also *Square Pegs*, chapter 1.

ries, birthdays, your kids' birthdays, your kids' school events. It seems counterproductive in the short run, but then the grand gesture you inevitably create in order to make up for it always fixes everything. Plus you'll probably get some.

4. Watch a lot of football and drink a lot of beer. Don't like beer? Don't like football? Learn. Taking up golf might be even better, because it gets you out of the house for hours, and nobody ever sees you doing it (just make sure to always use a golf cart, lest you inadvertently drop a few pounds from walking). You could be at a strip club for all anyone knows—and be sure to have a cover story in place about needing lots of singles to tip the caddy.

5. Complain about your wife to your friends a lot. It may seem disloyal, but your alternative is complaining about your wife to your wife, and that isn't going to get you anywhere.

6. Don't have any common interests. You're both just going to have to get used to the fact that you like beer, sports, and bowling, while your wife likes book club, talking, a clean house, nagging you, and your kids. Try to regularly find some time when neither of you is busy with your own pursuits to enjoy each other. And yes, her nagging you and you complaining about it does count. There are plenty of couples where that's all they ever do together.

7. No yard work. Yard work involves going outside, and the one thing that's never allowed on hot girl/ schlubby-guy sitcoms is going outside. The hot wife

may lay eyes on a man whose pants don't have elastic panels in them, and that simply won't do.

With these handy tips in mind, gentlemen, feel free to supersize.

THE TRUTH WILL OUT

One of the most important things to take away from television is that nobody ever gets away with lying. Ever. To anyone. Especially the other person in their relationship. Who, upon learning they've been deceived, is not likely to care much for the experience.

Sure, we all remember our parents telling us that honesty is the best policy. And we all nodded somberly and said we understood and we'd never tell a lie again. And we were lying when we said it.

But television teaches us that nobody ever gets away with anything more than the occasional innocuous untruth, especially protagonists. You'd think this is simply because TV characters are really, really terrible at lying, though never bad enough at it that the person they're lying to can actually tell.[5] And it happens *all* the time. The sequence of events is commonplace: for instance, on sitcoms, one character lies to another, either to stay out of trouble or to get away with doing something they're not

---

5. Unless that person is Jack Bauer on 24, who can always tell when someone's lying no matter how well they're doing it, probably because they always are, and if they weren't when Jack started questioning them, they sure as hell are (and now have been all along) by the time he finishes with them.

supposed to do or to get someone else to do something they wouldn't otherwise do. Over the course of the next half hour, the tale begins to unravel, and laughs are wrung from the liar's increasingly frantic attempts to keep the lie-ee (for lack of a better word) in the dark. Sometimes the lie-ee knows all along and is just enjoying watching the liar twist him- or herself in knots, and other times the lie-ee has no clue until the final scene. It's happened multiple times in just about every domestic sitcom you can think of, from *I Love Lucy* (Lucy lies to Ricky and ends up having a lot of 'splainin' to do) to *The Cosby Show* (one or more of the kids lies to Cliff so ineptly that Cliff has no choice but to set an elaborate trap for them) to just about the entire run of *Mad About You* (Paul lies to Jamie about some bonehead thing he did and ends up enlisting everyone they know to cover his ass) to *According to Jim* (Jim lies to . . . oh, who are we kidding, nobody watches *According to Jim*). In *The Sitcom Writers' Big Book of Stock Plots*,[6] "Lying" probably has an entire chapter to itself, if not an entire volume. And yet the message can always be boiled down to five words: *don't lie because you'll get caught*. Yes, I know that's six words. So I lied.

So let's say you've ignored all the warnings, disregarded fifty-odd years of televised cautionary tales about the dangers of anything short of scrupulous honesty, and told your significant other a lie. And let's take it as assumed that you have already recognized what a bonehead move that was. Now the question is: How much time do you have before you get caught?

Well, it depends on what kind of life you lead. If a normal day for you is like a wacky sitcom, you have a half hour at most

---

6. Not an actual title.

before you get busted. On the bright side, the consequences won't be as severe. All your panicked high jinks have burned up so much time that the victim of your dishonesty won't have a large enough window to do more than give you a brief lecture. At worst, you'll get chased around the living room sofa a few times.[7] Things may get more heated if your marriage is prone to long, uncomfortable bedtime conversations like on *Everybody Loves Raymond*, but you won't go to sleep mad or anything. And then the next time we see you, it will all have blown over.

Now, if your life is more like a nighttime soap opera, I'm sorry to say that you're in deep, deep trouble. The good news is that with the more protracted, serialized story lines of hour-long dramas, your day of reckoning is probably still weeks or even months away. Even so, a year is probably the best you can hope for. And especially look out for sweeps months like February and May. Those are always times for huge revelations, and the last thing you want is for one of those revelations to be about you. These are probably good times of the year to leave the country for a while, or consider having yourself recast.

A lie is like a house. Once it's up, you think it's finished. But then you have to live in it, and it isn't long before you—and the people you share it with—start noticing the parts of it that don't work. And then it's just a matter of time before it comes down around your ears and your long, long, Pinocchio nose.

But even before the shit hits the fan, it's not like your victim's months of blissful ignorance will be easy for you either. For instance, even when you have a moment to take some time off from covering your tracks and enjoying the company of that

---

7. And don't tell me you have your living-room sofa against the wall instead of out in the middle of the room like you're supposed to.

special person you're screwing over, they're constantly going to be going on about how wonderful and trustworthy and honest you are (which should be a red flag right there, because nobody ever says that unless they're being grievously deceived). And every one of these compliments will twist in your gut while you try and fail to smile happily and end up instead with an expression like you just started chemotherapy.

But it's not like you can do anything about it. Even if, after months of agonizing, you decide to do the right thing and tell the truth, you're still out of luck. That's because as soon as you resolve to go find and disabuse the person you deceived, like, right now, *that's* when they're going to find out the truth some other way. The most likely informer is some other person you've drawn into your web of deception, who either has their own attack of conscience or makes some kind of slip.

Which reminds me, if you're going to have a web of deception, don't draw someone else into it. Webs of deception are crowded enough as they are with only one person in them. Yes, you may think you need someone to talk to about this, so the two of you can chew it over from every possible angle and ensure that anyone listening or watching fully understands your not-completely-selfish motives, but that's just going to end up biting you in the ass. Think back to the time on *Ally McBeal* when Ally and Billy kissed, and then Ally tried to convince Billy not to confess to his wife (and Ally's friend), Georgia. Billy ended up telling the truth, and Ally ended up getting burned over it. You may think that Billy's relationship with his wife is the overriding priority here, but that's because you've forgotten that the show was called *Ally McBeal*. Which meant Billy's infidelity and subsequent confession to his wife were really all about Ally. Just like everything else was.

There are exceptions to every rule, naturally. There was the time on *Mad About You* when Paul accidentally gave his and Jamie's bed to charity, then got it back in pieces and made everyone come over to put it back together for him while he tried to stall her entry into the bedroom. The ruse worked, and she never suspected, even when the bed collapsed under her and then later when all of their friends sneaked out of the closet without disturbing the increasingly amorous Buchmans. So you might be okay, but only if you have friends like that.

And although it wasn't a lie between members of a romantic couple (terabytes of Internet fan-fiction notwithstanding), there's the infamous "Xander's Lie" on *Buffy the Vampire Slayer*. Xander was supposed to bring Buffy a message that Willow was working on a spell to make her ex-boyfriend Angel not evil again, but instead Xander just told her, "Kick his ass." Aside from a passing mention five seasons later, nothing ever came of it (although in an unrelated incident, Xander did eventually end up getting an eye gouged out. An eye for a lie, as it were).

But what kind of exceptions are those? Neither show was a consistent bastion of realism. *Buffy* dealt with vampires, werewolves, witches, and demons, and *Mad About You* was known to occasionally slip into parallel universes. So there you go.

Here's how you tell if you're being lied to: the person telling the lie will scrunch his face up, get all uncomfortable, stutter (which of course nobody on TV ever does unless they're either a guest character on a Very Special Episode or being played by Bob Newhart), and use a hundred words to answer a question where four would serve just as well. One evening, I walked in on the middle of an episode of *Grey's Anatomy* in which a group of interns was asking another intern, Alex, how things were going with his surgical mentor, Dr. Addison Montgomery-Shepherd. Alex's brain went into vapor lock while his mouth went into overdrive and his eyes flashed GUILTY in tiny little LEDs. The other interns—several of whom had either dated Alex in the past or were currently doing so, I'm certain—watched this display in confusion. I asked my wife, who had seen the whole episode thus far, "Alex is snogging Addison?" She quickly confirmed it, even though the allegedly brilliant surgical interns actually in the scene with Alex were completely clueless. And I didn't have any more information about the episode than I just gave you, with the possible exception of the fact that Dr. Addison Montgomery-Shepherd is a girl.

And by the way, if you're beginning to suspect that someone has lied to you as a result of some fact coming to light that just doesn't fit with their story? All you have to do is confront them with it. I'm not suggesting that they'll give up the tale and spill the truth immediately, because that won't happen. What they *will* do, and which is just as clear an indicator, is say, "I don't know what you're talking about." Then you'll know they're lying. Nobody ever says that otherwise. If someone actually is ignorant as to the accusation you're making, they will *ask*, "What are you talking about?" But making that flat statement signals an eagerness to get the conversation over with before they get busted. It also signals that they're kind of stupid, and you don't want to get fooled by somebody that dim-witted, do you?

TILL CANCELLATION DO US PART

TV is a great learning place for future couples, new couples, and couples who will be together forever (or at least until their show goes off the air, and for a minute there it looked like *The King of Queens* might be a near thing). But what about people who have already been through one marriage? What of the divorcé(e)s? Do they simply cease to exist?

Well, as a matter of fact, it depends on whether you're watching sitcoms or dramas. According to the sitcoms, you divorced folk are probably relegated to being costars at best.[8]

Divorce doesn't have quite the same stigma in the world of nighttime soaps, however. On certain hour-long dramas, some characters get divorced and leave the show faster than you can say "contract renegotiation." But watch your back; sometimes divorce takes too long, and it's deemed better to end a marriage by having a car drive over a cliff or by being in a church that gets shot up by terrorist commandos (*à la Dynasty*). Julie and Jimmy Cooper got divorced during the first season of *The O.C.*, and look how that turned out for Jimmy.

Now, there is one way to avoid divorce oblivion, and that is to shoot the moon. Which worked pretty well for Ross on *Friends*. When we originally met him, his first marriage

---

8. Even one of the most iconic shows in television history, *The Mary Tyler Moore Show*, was originally going to have Mary Richards as a divorcée striking out on her own. But back in the seventies, the network was too chickenshit to have such a progressive element as the foundation of one of its shows. I could go on about how Mary sure seemed to be starting over from square one for somebody who hadn't been through anything more devastating than a broken engagement, but the fact is that if the network hadn't been so terrified, *The Mary Tyler Moore Show* wouldn't have lasted two seasons and we never would have seen it again.

was just ending. His second marriage to Emily also ended in divorce a few seasons later—in fact, it was essentially over during the ceremony, when he accidentally called his bride Rachel. Sometime after that, he married Rachel herself in a drunken Vegas bacchanal that was regretted by both parties the moment the hangover started. And thus Ross scored a divorce hat trick. The lesson is that if you aren't any good at marriage—and plenty of people aren't—all you need to do is to compensate by just being really good at divorce. After all, look what happened to Ross's first two wives. They only got divorced one time each, and they're the ones who got phased out of the show. Rachel probably would have followed, if she hadn't gotten pregnant.

STANDING ON CEREMONY

There's a famous statistic that half of all marriages end in divorce. The corollary, of course, is that the other half end in death. On TV, *all* end in cancellation. Which is probably why people on TV work so hard to make their marriages succeed, and put up with shit week in and week out that would shatter lesser couples. They want to stay on the air.

Keep in mind, however, that even if some TV marriages last longer than they would in real life, the exact opposite is true of actual weddings. The first wedding I went to, I was expecting it to be a four or five-minute deal—ten minutes at the maximum— just long enough to fit neatly in between two commercial breaks. Imagine my chagrin at finding myself in a full-length Catholic mass. It was like having to go to church twice in one week.

Of course I could have been more prepared for my first real wedding if I had seen them on soap operas, in which the ceremony sometimes spans an entire weekend, beginning on Friday and concluding at about the same time on Monday. And everyone's wedding will be a jaw-droppingly lavish affair, even the ones thrown together at the last second. But then there is also the tension of spending the whole time waiting for the proceedings to be dramatically interrupted at a crucial moment by a cardiac event, jilted ex-lover, or the arrival of a presumed-dead spouse. Your wedding will be anticlimactic to say the very least if none of that stuff happens.

And the other thing about weddings I learned from TV? Apparently that whole "something old, something new, something borrowed, something blue" crap is crucial, as is the superstition about the groom not seeing the bride before the ceremony. No one seems concerned about when they're going to get everyone together for photographs; after all, why spend time filling a photo album when the images will be on thousands of TiVos all over the country by the time it's all over?

MULTIPLE CHOICE

If you've ever found yourself trying to balance things among three kids, try it with three adult women, as on *Big Love*, which follows the travails of Bill Henrickson and his three wives, a cautionary tale to any man who has ever fantasized about the life of a polygamist. It's clear that after a while, even sex becomes too much work. You'll find yourself hearing things like, "I'm your wife, but I'm also married to two other people. You forget that sometimes." Yeah, how dare you? And it's not like you'd get to make up for it with a lack of offspring; I'm not sure exactly how many children Bill has by Barb, Nicki, and Margene, but I think it's somewhere in the low sixties.

On the other hand, having three houses all in a row like that, all sharing one ginormous backyard? That would be sweet. But just for me and my one wife and my one kid. And maybe one room in one house could be occupied by the full-time handyman I'd need to take on, just for the upkeep of three separate structures. Totally worth it.

CONCLUSION

A lot of people spend as much as half of their lives being half of a couple. But you can be married to someone for fifty years and still be surprised at some of the stuff that pisses them off, even if it's the same stuff that pissed them off fifty years ago.

Ultimately, your best bet is to spend as much of your marriage in front of the TV as possible. Not only will you learn a lot in the process, but if all of your fights are over the remote, you'll be doing a lot better than most couples.

Learning Experiences

1 Cultivate a mutual attraction with a person of the opposite sex. Do your best to ensure that you remain unavailable to each other for as long as possible without ending the attraction or damaging the relationship. Keep practicing until you can do this for twenty years at a time, every time.

2 Men: Meet, woo, win, and marry a woman who is completely out of your league. Women: Allow yourself to be met, wooed, and married by a man out of whose league you totally are. Men: You're welcome.

3 Tell a lie to your significant other (claiming you completed this exercise doesn't count). Time how long it takes you to get caught. Whether you do so using a stopwatch or a calendar will tell you a great deal about your life.

4 If married, divorce your spouse. Afterward, keep close records to see which of you has more interesting things happen to you. If it's your spouse, you're not on the show anymore. And no, getting arrested for stalking doesn't count either.

4

What Would We Do,
Baby, Without Us?

Parenting

It can be scary and humbling to have some small,
helpless creature depending upon you for its very
existence. You want to avoid letting it down. You want
to do a good job for it. You want to make sure it has
everything it needs. Or at least you do if it's cute.

It would be inadvisable, to say the least, to jump
into any such caretaking situation without a great
deal of preparation. Fortunately, TV is there for you.
Which means that if you ever find yourself suddenly
responsible for a bunch of children like the star of *The
Bernie Mac Show*, all is not lost.

PRACTICE MAKES PERFECT

Television would have us believe that every high school, everywhere, has a unit in health class where they make each student responsible for an egg. The idea is to impress upon the kids the awesome burden of having to protect something as helpless and fragile as a child, which in turn is supposed to keep the girls from getting pregnant. Apparently educators believe there's no more effective anti-aphrodisiac for teens than the memory of a few days carting an egg around. These same educators fail to take into account the fact that there's also no more potent aphrodisiac than simply being a teenager.

My school actually never had this unit in its health classes. But that's okay, because I was able to get the gist from watching all the high school students on TV who had to go through it. And I'm pretty sure all my classmates did too, which I think is why I didn't get more action in high school. At least I tell myself that was the reason.

As is frequently the case, no series gets to the underlying truth of the egg-parent exercise better than *Buffy the Vampire Slayer*. In the episode "Bad Eggs," the students of Sunnydale High were issued items that looked like ordinary eggs, but in fact contained disguised alien parasites that crawled out of their shells, took over the bodies and minds of their hosts/parents, forced them to work in unending physical labor until they dropped, and turned them violently against those who truly loved them. Which is, of course, a lot more like having a child than just carrying around an egg for a week could ever be.

ANIMAL PLANET

For many people, the first small creature they're responsible for isn't a child at all, but an animal (I'm not judging any children's behavior here; I'm talking about actual, literal animals). You have to start somewhere. And don't worry, because as television is only too happy to tell you, any animal in your home is going to be smarter than you are.

I'm not just talking about Lassie, who was always so quick to run and alert the grown-ups that Timmy was stuck in the well. If Lassie had really been clever, she would have ditched that accident-prone kid in the woods and gotten herself a life of her own.[1] And I'm also not just talking all those cartoons where a bunch of idiot children or teenagers coalesce around some talking beast (the obviously puppettish Salem the cat on *Sabrina the Teenage Witch* very nearly falls into this latter category). And I am furthermore very much not thinking about Mr. Ed, who was admittedly smarter than Wilbur, who in turn was barely smarter than Ed's stall door.

I'm thinking, for one, about an early-eighties *Raiders of the Lost Ark* rip-off on ABC called *Tales of the Gold Monkey*. On that show, the 1930s pilot/adventurer played by Stephen Collins had as a sidekick a one-eyed terrier named Jack, who would bark once for no and two for yes, supposedly in the manner of all binary-question-answering dogs worldwide.[2] Lest you think this

---

1. An alternate theory is that the dog had Munchausen syndrome by proxy, and only hung out with Timmy so she could look like a hero by saving him all the time.

2. Not that this information was ever any use for me with the dogs I've met, because the show never went into what it means when a dog barks ten through several hundred times in succession.

little more than a novelty or a cute parlor trick, the guy would often ask the dog for advice. Kind of a risky proposition when zipping around over the South Pacific at a time in history when the Japanese were itching for an excuse to declare war on the United States. That's just asking for an international incident, not to mention an interspecies one. Still, Jack was a lot smarter than his owner. Not only was he demonstrably right most of the time; he had also, quite obviously for prime time broadcast television, never been fixed. A little terrier getting clearance to swing that thing around during the family hour clearly had plenty going on upstairs as well.

More supposedly high-minded shows fall into this trap as well. For instance, while almost everyone on *Frasier* was snooty, or sarcastic, or hypocritical, or self-aggrandizing, or Daphne, only Eddie the dog was none of the above. Yet somehow, in a show that had irony in just about every frame, Eddie could be completely arch just with a blank look or a well-timed exit from the room. He was the one who should have had his own radio show.

And as much as I meant to avoid cartoons, I have to make one exception for Brian on *The Family Guy*. The Griffins' dog has a world-weary monotone and a lot more perspective on any given issue than any of the humans do. Of course he also has a drinking problem, but considering that he lives with the Griffins, that's probably the smartest coping mechanism anybody could come up with. Just the fact that he's the only one who can un-derstand the psychotic rants of Baby Stewie is enough to keep him in a state of constant depression. Which brings us to the next section, in which we learn that Stewie may actually be one of the *less* malevolent and destructive members of his particular demographic.

OH, BABY

In addition to its many other useful qualities, television can be an effective birth-control device.[3] Even more, I would submit, than that ridiculous egg lesson. One of the ways it does this is with the obligatory diaper-changing scene. Television never bothers to start out showing us an experienced, efficient diaper changer on screen. It's always some neophyte who has somehow reached his (it's almost always a man) thirties without ever having to deal with a stinky. And despite television never showing the contents of said diaper, the reaction of the first-time diaper changer tells us more than a simple poop shot ever could.

In every case, the novice caregiver's initial reaction upon unwrapping Baby's Little Present is to recoil in horror, letting out some primal, wordless utterance of atavistic revulsion in the process. These scenes are always overplayed to the hilt, as if the actor has just punctured an adorable little perfumed water balloon that turned out to contain seven hundred pounds of raw sewage. The reality, of course, is much, much worse.

I was thirty-two years old before I found myself alone with a three-month-old who needed her poopy changed. Always anxious to avoid cliché, I steeled myself to suppress the terrified reaction that every TV first-timer allows himself to indulge in.

---

3. But only if you turn it on. And trying to use it in place of a condom or the pill will doom you to parenthood at best and permanent virginity at worst.

And then I opened things up, and I found out that that reaction is always shown for a reason: it is unsuppressible. TV gets it right again.

Newborn babies are in fact adorable little perfumed water balloons that contain *nine tons* of raw sewage at any given time. If you're very lucky, it'll only come out one ton at a time, and at least half of these expulsions will occur when the baby is wearing a properly applied diaper. But television did not prepare me for the spectacle of my two-month-old, feet in the air, expelling a horizontal brown geyser across the room. That certainly never happened on *Full House*.

Then, by the time television is done showing you the initial shock of fecal discovery, it leaves you with explicit instructions for coping with the ensuing situation: if you learn about diaper changing from television, you know that the best thing to do is to rummage around in panic for safety pins, try to fold a diaper like a cloth napkin at a fancy restaurant (even the disposable diapers), and end up with a kid dressed like a miniature, drunken Julius Caesar who will walk, crawl, or roll right out of the diaper the second you put him down.[4] And you will probably get peed on during the diaperless window of time. Your only means of rescue is the timely arrival of a properly qualified female, whose weary mocking you will gladly endure in lieu of having to deal with your wailing, wriggling Superfund site for one more second.

And the harried routine doesn't end there. Even after mom takes the kid away, you're left to deal with a room in total disarray. Now you're likely to step on a toy car and skate involuntarily across the room, bark your shin on a now-superflous baby gate,

---

4. Alarmingly, this even applies to children who cannot yet walk, crawl, or roll.

and inadvertently take a giant swig of bottled breast milk. When you finally sink exhausted into the couch, the impact of your ass will inevitably trigger a noisy, high-pitched protest from a squeaky toy under the cushions. Extra points if this is the self-same toy you've been searching for to calm an enraged tot for the last six hours.

And yet somehow it's all worth it the next time the infant smiles or coos at you. Especially if it's wearing a little hat, like they pretty much always are.

Because that's the other thing about babies. Either they can't talk, and are therefore unable to tell you what they need or where they hurt or what's going on in their soft little skulls, or they can, and are thus creepy as hell, like *Baby Bob*, and you just want to get them the hell away from you.

Somewhere in between we can find out what babies really think, and no, I'm not referring to *Look Who's Talking*. Babies are small and wee and helpless and totally dependent on us for their very existence on an hourly basis, and you just know they absolutely despise us for that. That's why I'm convinced that the most realistic reflection of the infant psyche is Stewie Griffin on (once again) *The Family Guy*. Being a cartoon and all, Stewie's got a football-shaped head, an inner monologue with the voice of a fifties horror movie villain, and a consuming hatred of all mankind. Only the dog talks to him; all of the verbal adults and teenagers who surround him are completely oblivious to his sociopathic ambitions, yet his every evil plan is invariably thwarted. And why? Just because he's a baby and nothing ever works out for him. I'm quite grateful to Stewie for warning me that when my infant son used to throw things out of his crib, he was actually trying to kill me.

Not all babies are like Stewie, however. He's been a baby since *The Family Guy* premiered in 1999, since cartoon children have a tendency not to age (see also Maggie Simpson, who is still crawling around in a layette with a pacifier screwed in tight despite being chronologically old enough to drink). There are some parents who prefer babies to older children. To those people, I would strongly advise them to give birth only to cartoons.

TODDLE ON

Having a baby gets easier when your child is no longer an infant. This is because you'll hardly ever see it anymore.

The message from TV is that the toddler years will pretty much take care of themselves, in the sense that there probably won't be any. From *I Love Lucy* to *Mad About You* to *Six Feet Under*, initially childless shows tend to disappear from the TV schedule as soon as the offspring begin to talk. If not sooner.

Maybe this has to do with child labor laws, or maybe it's more to do with the lead actors following an old vaudeville rule: never work with children or animals (or, for that matter, anything that fits both categories). Or maybe it's just a reflection of a certain TV writer's conceit. Theoretically, every scene on every television show has to have an objective where something has to happen, and anything that doesn't serve that objective needs to be excised. And as anyone who has ever spent any amount of time with a toddler is massively aware, they're really not focused on serving anyone else's objectives. Unless those objectives are to hear a long, protracted, slurred, digressive story about a fire engine and a spider, most TV shows do not have room for a toddler to toddle into the room and derail whatever intense proceedings are currently supposed to be riveting us to our seats. In many cases, we're worse off for it; we've all sat through any number of car chases, shoot-outs, and police interrogations that could have been vastly improved by the addition of a three-year-old wandering in to show everyone what's in her mouth.

But that's all a bunch of theory. The practical application to you and me is that once all the diaper-related hilarity has been totally milked out of the child, you can just about coast all the way to the teen years.

SAY GOOD NIGHT

As challenging as the daily grind of parenting may sometimes seem, you can always look forward to an end point. The time will come when you can freely have adult conversations with your fellow grown-ups without having to spell out every fifth word, in normal voices and at a leisurely pace while you crack open a beer. No, I'm not talking about when the kids go to college; I'm talking about when they go to bed.

If you're concerned that having a child will have a deleterious effect on your emotional or social life, not to worry: if your kids are anything like the ones most TV parents have, they'll be in bed the majority of the time. For instance, Nate on *Six Feet Under* was feeling completely trapped when his daughter Maya was born, but then *SFU*'s entire final season took place after Maya's bedtimes, so it was fine (until Nate died, that is, which put a whole new kind of cramp in his style). The Barones on *Everybody Loves Raymond* practically lived their entire marriage in long conversations before their own bedtime (and on rare occasions when their kids did show up on-screen, they were so quiet and still as to be mistaken for mannequins with crayons in their hands). In other words, don't be concerned that becoming responsible for another human life will affect your own all that much, because every time something interesting happens, they'll be asleep.

And as a bonus, you never have to have another fight with your significant other, because all the yelling will wake up the baby, and once you hear the angry crying from the other room cutting through your own recriminations, you and your partner are home free. Argument over.

YOU'VE GOT TO BE KIDDING

In very rare cases, an infant or toddler character will mature on-screen to the point where he or she is no longer required by law to be played by twins. What then happens is that the show has two child actors doing the work of one child actor. It puts them in the position of having to vie for attention in a perverse dynamic not unlike that of two siblings competing for the affection of a single parent, where the single parent is an eleven share in the Nielsen's. Worse yet, this by necessity occurs at a highly fragile and formative period of their lives. And then they end up turning into the Olsen twins. Obviously, this kind of situation is to be avoided at all costs.

More often, however, we're introduced to child characters after they've already grown old enough to speak. And therein lies a very real danger.

Nobody ever hears or uses the words *sass* or *backtalk* anymore. Is it because these are simply outmoded terms, or is it for the same reason that fish never say "water" (aside from the fact that fish can't talk, of course)? It's because TV tells both parents and kids that children making smart-ass comments at their parents' expense is and should be a standard mode of interaction.

So many sitcoms are built around families, and yet almost all sitcoms are also built around characters making sarcastic remarks to one another. How are both of these things possible? TV may teach us that it's okay to make a cutting, sarcastic remark to your parents, but my personal experience proved otherwise. Yet family sitcoms are full of kids saying things to their folks that I may have considered saying to mine at some point, but held back because it occurred to me that I might want to leave the house again someday.

The fact is that too many parents pick up a dangerous lesson from family sitcoms, and that lesson is this: smart-ass kids get to live. Too many of today's parents are letting their offspring treat them like straight men, because that's how TV tells them (and their children) to act. Except real parents don't even get Emmys or a laugh track, so here's the tragedy: that's *the wrong lesson*. The real lesson is that we teach people how to treat us. If we let them get away with something, they'll just keep doing it. Arnold Jackson, Alex P. Keaton, and the Soprano kids are cautionary tales of what can happen in the homes of parents who let their kids sharpen their wits on them.

That's why kids should be kept away from reruns of *Family Ties* and *Roseanne,* and be steered instead toward *The Cosby Show*. Cliff Huxtable's kids occasionally ventured the odd retort directed at their parents, but everyone in the house was fully aware that going into a battle of wits with Cliff was like going into a firefight unarmed. So maybe the lesson is that while you can occasionally let your kids have a little fun at your expense, make sure you're funnier.

THE TEEN YEARS

Things get tougher later on. In a few years, your kids will still be too young to smoke, drink, drive, do drugs, or have sex. Unfortunately, they won't know that. And you're going to have to be prepared for the moment when things get "very special."

We all know there are kids out there who get up to all manner of destructive behavior, going to wild make-out parties and listening to that rock-and-roll music and dancing the frug or what have you. You don't need to worry about your kid turning into one of those. Those kids are always someone else's. Like your child's best friend, who will be named "Boner" or "Cockroach" or "Six."

Now, that's not to say that your teen—the series regular, let's call him or her—won't come into contact with this species of hellcat. He or she will. It's only a matter of time. The only question then is how your impressionable young teen will handle the situation. Will he be the type to be so shocked at seeing an algebra classmate sucking on a Marlboro that he'll run home to you and confess his soul-crushing guilt at having merely witnessed such debauchery and promise never to do it again? Or will she topple into a spiral of self-destruction so vertiginous and abject that within a half hour she's gotten drunk and crashed your car?

Sad to say, it all depends on you and what kind of parent you are. If you're always up in your kid's business *7th Heaven* style, to the point where they can't sneak an extra cookie without getting caught, then they'll know it and eventually come clean. Sure, they'll jump through any number of hilarious hoops along the way in their desperate attempts to keep you in the dark, but a reckoning is inevitable. If you're *really* good, you knew the whole truth all along, a fact you'll reveal with some Columbo-like query just when they think they're out of the woods, like that time on *Cybill* when the kids borrowed her car. And in case anyone wonders whether your type of parent really means business, you can just point to *7th Heaven*'s poor Mary Camden, who was banished from the family for the unconscionable crime of drinking half a beer.[5]

If, on the other hand, the show is more about you than your kid, then Junior's probably going to register pretty low on your list of priorities for long periods of time. If you're distracted by, just for example, a hostile takeover under way at your work-place, your affair with your sister-in-law, a relative who wants to kill you, and/or an evil twin who keeps fucking up your credit, your kid's going to get away with a lot before you get involved. I realize you have your own stuff going on, but take a moment to make sure your car insurance is paid up. And make friends with a lawyer if you have time.

The other alternative, of course, is that you're not even around, and your kid is one of those "other people's kids" I was talking about earlier. But if everyone is the star of their own se-ries, it's probably a good idea to have a regular speaking part in

---

5. I didn't actually see this episode, but heard about it secondhand. So at first I thought that Mary had gotten into trouble for wasting the other half of the beer. I'm not saying I would kick my kid out for that; at worst, it's a grounding offense.

your kid's show. Being in the opening credits is ideal. If you can swing that, your kids will be fine. Sure, one of them might get temporarily recast like on *Roseanne*, but families have survived worse than that. They have to, because they're families. And also because there are probably contracts involved.

Just think about how you would react if someone moved into your house and took over the whole place and your entire life just eating, sleeping, crapping and peeing all over everything, and waking you up several times a night. We put up with it from our babies because they're tiny and helpless and cute. Adult guests, of course, can't get away with this type of behavior, no matter how hard some of them might try. But when the adult in question is the same one you didn't kill for tipping over your china cabinet when he was eight months old, you really can't kill him for burning your house down now.

I should now insert the disclaimer that all of the reassurances in this section are null and void if you're on an HBO series, in which case your kid is a dim-witted future hood like A. J. Soprano or a druggie with completely self-destructive taste in boys like Claire Fisher from *Six Feet Under*. But then if you're on HBO, you're already so screwed in so many other ways you probably won't have time to worry about your kids at all.

FAMILY STRUCTURE

Think about the family you grew up with. Were your mother and father married? To each other? Had they always been married to each other, even before you were born? Did you have one or more siblings? If so, did those siblings also have both of the same parents that you did? Were your parents married before *they* were born, even if your siblings are older? And if the answer to all of these questions is yes, how were you able to understand what traffic lights were telling you when everything was in black and white?

I'm being facetious, of course, because I recognize that by the fifties you could see color simply by going to the movies. But by the time I was growing up in my own traditional nuclear family, the similarly structured familial units of *Father Knows Best* and *Leave It to Beaver* already seemed quaint, not to say outdated. *The Brady Bunch* was already in syndicated reruns by the time I was receiving its positive message of how blended families can not only make it work, but meld together so seamlessly that the only indicators as to who started where was their gender and hair color. And it doesn't seem like the first regular series about a single dad could have been all that long ago, but just try getting a show called *The Courtship of Eddie's Father* on the air these days and you'll probably end up on *Dateline*.

So many shows are built on the high concept of a nontraditional family structure, like single dad / kids / domestic employee (*Diff'rent Strokes, Gimme a Break, The Nanny, Frasier*); single mom / kids / domestic employee (*Who's the Boss, Murphy Brown, Kate & Allie* if you count one of the two single moms as a domestic employee); blended families (*The Brady Bunch, Once and Again, Step by Step, Big Love . . .* sort of); interracial adoptions (*Webster, Diff'rent Strokes* again); bachelors-turned-reluctant-fathers (*My Two Dads, Two and a Half Men*); and divorce (too numerous to mention) that sitcoms about more "traditional" families have nearly become anachronisms, like *Family Ties, Growing Pains,* and *Roseanne*. Which aren't even on anymore, so there. The "nuclear" family has more varieties of nucleus than the Periodic Table of Elements does.

What this should have taught any astute viewer by now is not to assume you know everything about someone's home life simply by applying the template of the widely recognized "nuclear" structure. And yet we still get to see people on TV making fools of themselves, assuming that everyone who lives in one house has the same last name, or getting a kid on the phone and asking, "Is your mom home?" or "Is your dad home?" In the latter case, the ignorant caller usually learns that mom is somewhere in Arizona on the second year of a three-year bender or dad was abducted by aliens. Depending, of course, on which parent is being requested. And we still see teachers at parent-teacher conferences assuming that any older adult accompanying or representing a student is an actual biological parent, and not an adopted parent, stepparent, aunt, uncle, grandparent, sibling, domestic employee, band manager, CIA handler, or what have you. You'd think that teachers, more than anyone, would have learned by now not to assume that parent-teacher conferences are attended by only parents and teachers. But they never fail to act all confused or, in some cases, even judgmental about Junior's home situation. This may temporarily embarrass the family, but they're just going to come back at you stronger and more indignant, probably ripping a strip off you in the process just for acting like such an ignorant jackhole.

Which may be the most important lesson of this entire chapter: not to be that particular kind of ignorant jackhole.

CONCLUSION

Parenting really isn't as hard as television tends to make it out to be; it's much, much harder. At least until someone invents a remote control with a "clean your room" button right next to "mute" (and gets the mute button to work, while they're at it).

Learning Experiences

1 Challenge your pet to a battle of wits. If you win, have your pet euthanized immediately.

2 Carry an egg around for a week and pretend to be its parent. If you're out of high school and anyone asks you why you're so far behind the times, ditch the egg and get a Tamagotchi.

3 Change a baby's diaper. If you don't have access to a baby, change your own diaper. A full written report, with footnotes and photographs, will be grounds for immediate disqualification.

4 Father, birth, or adopt a child. Raise him or her to adulthood, helping your child to avoid whenever possible such common pitfalls as bad grades, disobedience, lying, bullying, drug use, brushes with the law, and death. Consider this task completed when your fully grown child tells you what a great parent you were. And then write your own damn book.

5

Making a Living

The Workplace

Many people work because they have to, not because they want to. It's a way to pay the bills, to keep the kids in new outfits and fresh hair-cuts every week, and to keep the house-set scenery standing up straight. It can be frustrating, stressful, and misery making, and it doesn't help that even the thought of losing a job you hate can be terrifying to some people. So, many people come home from a long day at work, settle down in front of the TV, and escape into a show that's set . . . in the workplace.

THE TV WORKFORCE

As kids grow up, they get their ideas of what they want to be when they grow up from watching TV. So they want to be police officers, or doctors, or firemen (at least they do until they get old enough to watch *NYPD Blue*, *House*, or *Rescue Me*), or superheroes. Often all at the same time.

As they get older, they learn that not everyone can have those jobs; there are only so many of them, and they're kind of hard to get and even harder to do. So they start looking beyond the TV screen for potential careers, and instead start thinking that maybe they'd rather be TV actors, screenwriters, directors, or stuntmen. It's all part of growing up.

So clearly, the jobs people do on TV can't match the jobs people do in real life. Let's assume for a moment that if you were to break down TV characters by profession, you would get an accurate reflection of the country's actual workforce. By this logic, the largest single profession would be police officers and other investigators of crime.[1] They would be closely followed by doctors and nurses. A surprisingly large percentage would be freelance entrepreneurs of some kind or another, whether they be aspiring restaurateurs, industrialists, fugitives, or superheroes.

Now, based on what we know about the people in these professions from TV, they're always going on about how much the job demands of them, and indeed we always see them working inhuman hours to put this week's scumbag behind bars/save a victim of an horrific injury/chase down a bad guy who absorbs other people's superpowers by eating their brains. So clearly people in these professions have negligible home or personal lives. How this could be the case when there are so very many of them is beyond me; they should all be fighting over the limited

---

1. See chapter 7, "Don't Do the Crime If You Can't Do the Time."

amount of work there would be to go around in these fields, like the interns on *Grey's Anatomy* do all the time.

That's why, out of all the hundreds of regular TV characters out there right now, only a very small percentage are office drones toiling away at a sad little company somewhere in Middle America.[2] And before *The Office* came to NBC, there were hardly any. Plenty of TV characters have waited tables or tended bar—especially high-school- and college-student characters that producers could put into cute uniforms, *à la Dawson's Creek* or *Beverly Hills 90210*—but they haven't been the whole focus of a show since *Alice* and *Cheers* went off the air (which is surprising, considering how many actors out there have real-life experience in this area).

The news media in our world would have us believe that the people in the workforce with less personal time than anyone are software developers, who live in a constant state of "crunch" time, sleeping under their desks, subsisting on what they can scrounge out of vending machines and other people's pizza boxes, while rocking an office wardrobe that's built entirely around ill-fitting product-launch T-shirts. But TV tells us that isn't the case. For one thing, there's no such thing as software developers in TV, and for another, all the software that people use is either total crap or impossible magicware that could only have been coded by elves with Cold Fusion.[3] So you do the math.

Whereas on TV, the only people who have ever come clos-

---

2. The 2007 season did significantly up the number of retail-service employees, however, with *Chuck* and *Reaper*. But even those guys have second jobs working for the CIA and the Devil, respectively, which presumably most of their real-life counterparts do not. If they do, I need to remember to be more patient when I'm waiting for someone to sell me a washing machine.

3. See chapter 10, "Surfing on the Internet and Zapped to Cyberspace."

est to such punishing schedules are the poor suckers on *The West Wing*. They seemed to spend twenty hours a day inside the White House—except for the president, who actually lived there. There was one episode where Josh "magnanimously" sent Donna home at 11 p.m., on the condition that she come in early the next day to make up for it. And since a later episode showed Josh hauling himself out of bed to make coffee at 4 a.m., it's not that hard to figure out how much sleep Josh was used to getting, which goes a long way toward explaining why he was kind of an asshole a lot of the time.

The point is that when you're picking a career, the amount of time you expect to have to yourself is clearly an important factor. If you don't mind spending all your time at work, be a cop or a doctor or a highly ranked administration official.[4] Otherwise, choose a career that can be relied upon to get you home on time, like a bus driver (*The Honeymooners*), documentary filmmaker (*Mad About You*), or obstetrician (*The Cosby Show*). That way you can spend more time being driven crazy by your wife and kids for free, instead of by the people who pay you to let them drive you crazy.

Okay, now I'm rethinking this. Maybe it isn't so much about finding a balance between work and home as it is deciding which one of the two areas your life focuses on. If you're on a show where you spend most of your time at home with your family, good for you. But this chapter's done with you, because it's about the workplace. And no, the time you spend at home watching TV shows about other people's workplaces doesn't count.

---

4. Who, I suspect, aren't simply speaking under condition of anonymity as much as the media might claim; they're just too tired to remember their own names.

THE GRASS IS ALWAYS GREENER ON THIS
SIDE OF THE TUBE

People don't just use TV to escape. They also like to see shows that reflect their daily reality, and they probably appreciate even more seeing shows about people who are more miserable at work than they are. This is probably why different versions of *The Office* have been successful in four different countries. All of us have had a nightmare boss, or, if you don't now, you did in the past. And if you don't now *and* you never have, you're in for some very unpleasant work experiences further down the road.

As bad as David Brent/Michael Scott/the Canadian guy/the French guy on the various versions of *The Office* are, they aren't the worst bosses in the world (only one of the four could possibly hold that distinction, anyway). Sure, they're self-aggrandizing, condescending, ignorant pricks who always think they're the funniest guy in the room. But at least they try to be friendly sometimes. Other TV bosses, like Mr. Wick on *The Drew Carey Show* (and his invisible, phone-bound predecessor) actually were funny, but since they directed their mean-spirited humor at their underlings, who didn't typically find it funny, it was more of a net loss for the employees.

There's also an office weirdo everywhere you work. On the U.S. version of *The Office*, it's Dwight, the humorless fascist, with his nerdy tastes in entertainment, his self-proclaimed status as a volunteer sheriff's deputy, and his work wardrobe whose color palette is composed entirely of puke tones. On *The West Wing*, it's Leo's tightly wound assistant, Margaret, who can't even tell a joke without looking like she's about to pop a vein. Sometimes there's even more than one, as on *Taxi*, where unkempt burn-out Reverend Jim filled the role anytime nutty foreigner Latka wasn't around (because Andy Kaufman was off doing something even weirder in real life during that week's shooting). And on *Ed*, there were at least two weirdos working at the show's central setting, Stuckey Bowl (which also served as Ed's law office): Phil (the constant huckster goofy enough to end up as a regular on VH-1's *I Love . . .* series) and Shirley (who made *The West Wing*'s Margaret look like a laid-back stoner). And you could probably also make a case for Kenny (a hulking bruiser with a degree from Tufts), not to mention Ed himself, because . . . come on. A bowling-alley lawyer who denied being a bowling-alley lawyer? How many of those do you know?

Not that the office weirdo position isn't sometimes hotly contested. In one episode of *NewsRadio*, WNYX's resident weirdo Matthew felt distinctly threatened by a weird temp played by French Stewart. Even the temp was aware of the tension, and himself saw Matthew as a rival for the single slot of "weird guy." It all rang a bit false to me. Having worked many jobs in many offices with many people over the years, I can say that working in an office with only one weird guy[5] would have been a nice break. For instance, the guy who did a bit of mime for me every time he passed my desk was bad enough. The guy who thought he was connected to the Mob was bad enough. Working with them both at the same time was kind of hard to take.

---

5. Counting those other than myself.

WHAT'S MY JOB AGAIN?

But then, at a TV workplace, you only have to remember the names of five or six people (even if you would think it takes many times that number to operate an actual radio station, newsroom, advertising agency, law firm, hospital, or cruise ship). Obviously TV characters are masters at multitasking. They only get a limited window of existence each week, so it's to their definite advantage to get as much done during this time as possible. Doing *more* than is possible is even better. Hence on any given hour of *24*, Chloe might act as an intelligence analyst, IT specialist, computer repair person, receptionist, and dispenser of unsolicited personal advice. There were a couple of episodes in which she also got to shoot people, but in light of Chloe's complete lack of social skills, I'd say they got off lucky by not having to interact with her face-to-face.

Even more mysterious are those with the ability not only to do two jobs at once, but to do the same job in *two places* at once. For years, I wondered how Isaac on *The Love Boat* knew whether on any given shift he was supposed to be running the main bar topside in his red bartender's jacket (which must have been sweltering under the tropical sun, despite whatever protection might have been offered by the shade of his Afro), or the belowdecks bar in his black vest and billowy pirate shirt. It was such a relief when I finally realized he was doing both at the same time, twenty-four hours a day. Probably less of a relief for him, though.

Plus he was always manning both bars by himself, as well as serving as a poolside waiter most of the time, carrying trays to deck chairs when he wasn't mixing drinks for five hundred passengers behind the counter (or possibly, thanks to the magic of editing, even when he was). Adding to his problems must have been the fact that bartenders in popular media are expected to be dispensers of advice, and nowhere would such advice be needed more than on a cruise ship full of lovelorn morons. Yet after Isaac had delivered his fruity frozen drinks with a beaming smile and a jaunty double-handed point, he generally had to confine himself to making noncommittal expressions once the heavy discussion started. Maybe network TV audiences in the 1970s just weren't ready to see a black man telling white people what to do on Saturday nights.

But then there were advantages to Isaac's gigs as well. No rush home, for one. Free alcohol, for another. Finally, and perhaps most significantly, if Isaac had ever taken more than a few minutes off at a time, he would almost certainly have strangled Gopher.

OFFICE ROMANCES

It's fairly common knowledge that it's not a good idea to date someone you work with. It's not common knowledge on TV, though, where coworkers are always getting involved with one another. Consider Pam and Jim's relationship on NBC's *The Office*. But then the same show has any number of other couples: Dwight and Angela (later, Andy and Angela), Ryan and Kelly, (later, Darryl and Kelly), and Michael and Jan. And that's not even counting Phyllis and her husband who works in the same building, Bob Vance of Vance Refrigeration. Those who haven't already paired off had better hurry up before it's too late and office lush Meredith gets snapped up by Creed.

In fact, for all the conventional wisdom that tells us not to date coworkers, the opposite message is typically conveyed by television. And it's easy to see why. Look at *Grey's Anatomy*. Except for the Chief's marriage (intermittently over), Dr. Bailey's marriage (over), and Meredith's brief partnering with a veterinarian (very much over), those people never get together with anyone they don't work with. And just look at how well that seems to be working out for them.

HAPPY MEDIA

The first and last (and in many cases, the only useful) advice many writers get is to "write what you know." So is it any surprise that there's so much TV about TV? Not to mention TV about other mass media that are powered by writers? Television is an art form, even if it's sometimes a lazy one. And if the purpose of art is to hold a mirror up to life, what could be lazier than holding the mirror up to oneself? Most of us find that more interesting anyway, and there's no reason television should be different.

TV shows about the media don't confine themselves to TV itself, however. There have been any number of shows set at radio stations, newspapers, magazines, and advertising agencies, not to mention the offices of novelists and comic-strip artists. And that's just the shows that have these arenas as their main focus, excluding the ones where they serve as subplots. For instance, we could go into Joey's on-again, off-again gig on *Days of Our Lives* during his run on *Friends*. But I don't want to.

ON THE AIR

Television hadn't even been around all that long before we had a television show about the making of a television show. Nobody in this world ever saw more than a few seconds of *The Alan Brady Show*, but in the world that exists inside the TV, it must have been a pretty big hit. It lasted even longer than *The Dick Van Dyke Show*, the sitcom about Alan Brady's writing staff. And Brady himself was still a comedy legend decades later, when Paul got to meet him in an episode of *Mad About You*. Both incarnations of Brady were portrayed by actual TV comedy legend Carl Reiner, most recently seen in the films *Ocean's 11–13*. No doubt a future *Ocean's* installment will find Reiner's character, Saul, pulling a con wherein he poses as comedy legend Alan Brady.

But we're getting ahead of ourselves. *The Dick Van Dyke Show* spent an awful lot of time in the writers' room with Rob, Buddy, and Sally, three comedy vets who at times seemed fresh out of vaudeville. They were performers as well as writers, more often than not producing their sketches by acting them out for one another rather than doing something as prosaic as writing them down. Even when Rob had his coworkers over to dinner at the house, there was always a better-than-even chance that some form of musical theater would break out. With these three constantly cutting up with their A-material behind the scenes, how could the show they were writing have been anything but brilliant? If they'd ever gotten any work done, that is. What we learned from this show is that in order to succeed as a TV writer, you have to have so much creativity bursting from your every pore that even writing comedy for forty hours a week still leaves you needing some kind of additional creative outlet. It's not surprising that Rob and Buddy and Sally had more material than they could ever get on the show. What I can't understand is that, as TV writers in a more innocent age, the stuff they wouldn't have been able to get on the air and thus had to share with one another should have been absolutely *filthy*.

Sometime after *Dick Van Dyke*, the actress who played Rob's wife, Laura, got a sitcom of her own about the making of a TV show. Except that in keeping with the theme of a woman starting over on her own, instead of a big hit comedy/variety show (back when there still were such things), Mary Tyler Moore got stuck helping put together a crappy little local newscast in a small Midwestern market. And by the way, I've lived in Minneapolis almost my whole life, and there has never been a TV station called WJM.[6]

When a young, fresh-faced Mary Richards presented herself at the desk of grumpy boss Lou Grant on *The Mary Tyler Moore Show*, she didn't have much going for her but spunk, which Mr. Grant now-famously hated. Yet she landed a gig at the WJM newsroom anyway, and worked her way up until she and everyone else (save Ted) got fired seven years later. There's still much to learn from these old reruns, however, like the fact that although local newscasts now tend to have fancy sets and animated graphics, there didn't used to be anything going on at that level except a guy like Ted Baxter in a plaid suit standing in front of a blue wall holding a sheaf of papers that he misread while rocking back and forth on his heels. It's no wonder everyone bemoans the state of local news these days; they spend too much time doing stuff like making the station's logo and call letters

---

6. The place was so cheap it only had three call letters.

seem to fly out of the screen at you, and less time actually reading the news in a really deep voice.

TV came out from behind the scenes in the eighties and nineties and moved on to TV personalities. Which is kind of a peculiar thing to have to say in light of the fact that the entire cast of *Murphy Brown* put together had less personality than Sally from *The Dick Van Dyke Show* all by herself. Somewhere, in between Murphy's culture-war skirmishes, we were able to glean that putting on a news-magazine show like *60 Minutes* or *20/20* or *Dateline* is both easier and harder than it looks. In one episode, when executive producer Miles got another show to run, everyone assured him that they could run *FYI* by themselves after years of practice. And then the first show without him was a near disaster, saved only by Miles's showing up mere seconds before airtime and barking out the precise series of orders that caused the show to go off without a hitch. Even after that success, and after demonstrating how necessary his expertise really was on the set, Miles decided to ditch his other show so he could keep concentrating on his first priority, *FYI*. If only Joss Whedon—who in one season had three series on the air (*Buffy the Vampire Slayer*, *Angel*, and *Firefly*) and a comic-book series in production—had seen that episode, much heartache could have been prevented for all concerned.

But if more than one show by the same creator is a recipe for disaster, then more than one show about the same thing—at the same time—is a recipe for something else. And that something else is enlightenment.

In the 2006–2007 season, NBC aired not one but two behind-the-scenes series about fake late-night sketch comedy shows and the wacky goings-on at the studio and the network offices. One, *Studio 60 on the Sunset Strip*, was created by Aaron Sorkin, who had already demonstrated an uncanny ability to teach us more about the U.S. government in any given episode of *The West Wing* than most of us could have possibly remembered from an entire school year's worth of social studies classes. Surely a man who had been making good TV since 1998 (also counting *Sports Night*) could make an educational hour of programming on the subject?

Except that the other show, the more economically named *30 Rock*, was a behind-the-scenes show about a fake late-night sketch-comedy show made by Tina Fey, who had spent years behind the scenes (as well as in front of them) on a real late-night sketch-comedy show called *Saturday Night Live*. So which of the two shows ended up being more reliably educational?

The safest way to judge is probably by looking at which of the two shows lasted longer. True, *Studio 60*'s first season did extend into the summer as a result of the network not wanting to broadcast the last few episodes at a time of year when people might watch them. But *30 Rock* is the one that got picked up for another year. So it's clearly the more trustworthy source of knowledge than its counterpart.

For instance, we already know that just like on *30 Rock*, there's a real-life network called NBC, as opposed to the fictitious NBS on *Studio 60*. By this logic, we can probably also assume that the backstage of a late-night sketch comedy show is populated not by recovering drug addicts, born-again comedians, and visiting *Vanity Fair* writers (as on *Studio 60*), but by goofy pages, hot assistants, and comedians and writers who are actually funny (as on *30 Rock*). However, since each show features a network honcho named Jack, each of whom is a deceptively hard-nosed bossy pants with a secret soft spot for some of his respective show's other characters, that's probably something you can take to the bank.

In the end, working on TV isn't any more glamorous than any other job. We need only look at *Family Ties* and Steven Keaton's job as a public-TV station manager to see that. There's nothing more inherently exciting about working on a TV show than there is about working on an assembly line, or in a restaurant, or in a brokerage firm. Except when there is, which, granted, is most of the time.

CAN YOU HEAR ME?

TV shows don't concentrate on television as the only medium, of course. It just thinks it's the best one. There have been plenty of shows about people who work in radio, and as sad and desperate as TV workers can be, at least they can count their blessings that they're not on the radio.

WKRP in Cincinnati, for instance, shows us what it's like to work at a sad little fourteenth-place rock station in a medium-size market. And it really should be in sixteenth place. For one thing, it only has four on-air personalities that we ever get to see: the perpetually hungover Dr. Johnny Fever, Venus Flytrap, that unctuous guy in the tennis sweater who was in, like, one episode (and who later ended up trapped on a mysterious island on *Lost*), and Les Nessman. I don't remember the last time I heard a rock station with its own dedicated news guy, particularly one so very obsessed with hog reports. Still, program director Andy Travis was bitterly disappointed when the Arbitron[7] ratings came out

---

7. Needless to say, *WKRP* also taught me what program directors do and what an Arbitron book is. Arbitron tells you how many people are listening to your radio station. The program director is the guy who gets pissy when the Arbitron book doesn't say what he wants it to.

and he wasn't at a number one station for the first time in his career. But I'd be willing to bet that even if there had been a spin-off about WKRP's longtime rival station, the higher-rated WPIG, we'd be hearing all the time about how they wanted to get out of radio and into TV. But then such a spin-off never could have happened, because in the days before media conglomeration, it took a group of people larger than a sitcom cast to run a top-rated radio station.

That's something I learned from *Frasier*. KACL, the Seattle talk station that broadcast the title character's call-in radio show, was a much larger radio ecosystem than WKRP. It also works as a model for AM-radio success: give a show to a fey wine and food critic, then follow him up with a self-important shrink, and then follow *that* guy with Bulldog the sports clown. Even if this combination of lead-ins doesn't make for boffo Arbitron ratings (which, how could it not?) it'll be worth it just to watch the tight-assed psychologist roll his eyes every time Bulldog obnoxiously rolls his cart full of sound effects into the studio while the shrink is still on the air. It takes a lot of people we never see to keep the station running, and those people are going to need some kind of entertainment.

Yet a third model is in place at WNYX, the New York–based, all-news station on *NewsRadio*. Most days start with a "staff meeting," which consists of all of the regular speaking roles and no one else. First of all, one can't help feeling some sympathy for the people bustling around in the background during these scenes, when the whole "senior staff" is gathered around that one table in the middle of the newsroom in plain view of everyone. Not getting invited to those meetings is enough of a slight. But having to see Beth the kooky admin and Matthew the goofball reporter acting like they belong there when you don't? That must be too much to bear. Maybe that's why we never saw any of the same extras in the background more than once. And second of all, if everyone is in a staff meeting, who the hell is on the air?

I kid, of course. It's not like the station couldn't continue operating without them. In the episode where Matthew was trying to organize a vacation house for everyone in the cast to go to for a week, everyone kept getting hung up on logistical details like who would get which bedroom and whether Bill would be allowed to wear his Speedo. Nobody ever asked how the station was going to stay on the air, whether it was going to be by rerunning a week's worth of news or recording an upcoming week's worth of news in advance. The only possible solution is that the station would continue as normal under the stewardship of the nonspeaking roles. Which, considering how little work we ever see any of the cast members do, is probably how it usually is anyway.

SEE YOU IN THE FUNNY PAPERS

According to TV, a surprisingly viable career option is that of syndicated comic-strip artist. It's clear why this is a tempting subject matter for a TV show. Comics writers must be pretty funny, since they write comics and everything, right? Plus, there's no need for both a home set and a work set, because they can work at home. Wait, now suddenly *I* want to be a comics writer.

The earliest example I can think of was Henry Rush on *Too Close for Comfort*, who was so confident in his drawing abilities that he used to draw his strip with a puppet of his character, Cosmic Cow, over his pen hand. Or maybe that was just there as a constant reminder to himself that with all the merchandising money pouring in, he'd better keep the crappy art pouring out.

Years later, Caroline on *Caroline in the City* was so unconfident in her drawing ability that either she or her syndicate—I can't remember which—brought an actual artist on board to help her do the coloring. Given that most newspaper strips only get colored in one day per week, I'm not sure how he made a full-time job out of it, unless Caroline's strip (titled, coincidentally, *Caroline in the City*) got a lot more space in the comics section than most do these days. Also, the two main characters hated each other. Which means, of course, they would eventually end up together, thereby killing the show (though not soon enough). Another reason to avoid office romance: it'll get you canceled. As we also learned from that show, sometimes artists can do a whole week's strips in one day and then take the rest of the week off. If it's really that easy, why don't more comic artists just have five to seven strips in the paper all the time? More than the ones who already do, that is.

There's still a lot of fertile educational ground to cover in this area, I think. Just look at your local paper's comics page, which probably still runs daily strips by deceased artists like Charles Schulz (*Peanuts*) and Johnny Hart (*B.C.*). What I'd like to see is a show that lets us in on how people continue to consistently get their work in the funny papers even when they're dead.

STOP THE PRESSES

In the eighties, we saw what it was like to work at a daily newspaper on *Lou Grant*, starring, shockingly enough, Ed Asner as Lou Grant. Apparently in those days, if you worked as an editor or a reporter, you spent most of your time grappling with journalistic ethical dilemmas. How far are you willing to go to get the story? What are you willing to print? How can you protect your sources? Such questions today would probably seem quaint; the big questions are likely to be more along the lines of, how will this increase circulation? Or, which giant media conglomerate is buying us out this week? Or, do you have any sticky interactive ideas to attract eyeballs for the online edition?

The problem with a daily newspaper, though, is that it's just too fast-paced an environment for a one-hour TV show to go into in any depth. A much more suitably paced environment is a monthly magazine. And, as we saw from shows like *Suddenly Susan* and *Just Shoot Me*, they're also good for attracting a more female-skewing audience.

Fashion magazines like *Blush*, the periodical whose offices were the setting of *Just Shoot Me*, are supposedly on a cycle that's six months ahead of their actual publication. To someone like me, to whom *fashion forward* means being aware of a trend less than a year after it's over, this kind of institutional prescience is mind-boggling. One might think that the only way they could possibly pull something like this off is by time travel, or magic, or having a huge staff of highly talented prognosticators. But it seems that instead all you need is a sixtysomething male editor in chief, his daughter, a sarcastic assistant, a photographer, and an ex-model. Never mind that there's more real-world journalistic experience than that in any high school newspaper (especially if that newspaper is the *Smallville Torch* on *Smallville* and Chloe is there alone). Yet somehow they managed to regularly put out not only a magazine, but one with cover headlines that could be used as scene interstitials because they were tangentially relevant to what was happening with the characters. How they consistently accomplished *that* six months in advance is nothing short of a miracle.

Of course one of the most successful magazine-set shows currently on the air in America doesn't, in a sense, even come from America (although that is its star's first name). Before *Ugly Betty* became a huge hit and won multiple Emmys, whoever would have thought that a show about a dumpy protagonist trying to make it in the fashion industry could ever succeed here, no matter how well it had done in other countries? Sure, *La Fea Mas Bella* did well in Mexico, and *Bette la Fea* was a hit in Venezuela, and *Verkekte Beti* won over Israel, and *Biti Yuki Yuki* took over Zimbabwe, and on and on through the entire U.N., but why should anyone have thought people here in the United States would go for it? Maybe it's a way of assuaging our guilt over being part of a shallow, "looks-ist" culture. If we can spend an hour each week rooting for a young woman who isn't conventionally attractive to succeed in a superficial industry like the fashion press, we can, with a clear conscience, blow off the people who aren't conventionally attractive in our everyday lives. Which becomes a big time-saver, since there are a lot more of them at our workplaces than there are in the TV.

Ugly Betty admittedly hasn't taught us much about the nuts and bolts of the fashion publishing biz, like how to work a printing press or how to sell millions of people 210 pages of ads with a straight face. But what it has taught us is that success in publishing is not about how good you are at your job or how much you love the magazine. It's really about who you know and whose son you are. The editor in chief of *Mode* magazine (and let's not even get into that title, which confused me for weeks because I thought that was still the title of a fashion magazine for plus-size women) is inexperienced, callow, ignorant of the industry, and a total man-whore. He's also the son of the publisher.

Whereas the creative director of *Mode* magazine is a brilliant strategist with drive, ambition, political acumen, and a keenly discriminating eye. She has dedicated herself to the magazine, to the detriment of her personal life. Yet this is obviously not the way to get ahead. Wilhelmina is hiss-worthy by virtue of the fact that she's kind of sneaky and scheming. Well, can you blame her? Clearly, just being good at her job didn't get her named to the top spot, which instead went to the publisher's idiot son. Who wouldn't have adopted some questionable tactics after that? Not that Wilhelmina should ever have thought she had a shot at running the place with the boss's kid around. Didn't she ever watch *Just Shoot Me?*

BY THE BOOK

Television loves writers. Actually, let me clarify that. Television *writers* love writers. Television itself would probably do without writers entirely if it could, and between the rise of reality TV and the occasional strike, it's been trying to for years. But since it can only do so to a certain extent, there are still plenty of writers able to put writers on TV. It's "write what you know" all over again. Which means the writers on TV can probably teach us more about real writers than the members of any other profession can teach us about theirs. It's depressing to realize that compared to what we can learn about writers from Rob Petrie, the percentage of trustworthy information we can learn about Kryptonians from Clark Kent is probably a smidge lower. So let's stay on the positive side of that comparison for now.

One teledidactic advantage of having writers as characters is that they can narrate the proceedings in voice-over, offering ostensibly literate real-time insight on the plot and characters. Even though many writers regard this as a cheap expository device, some still can't resist the lure of a literate-sounding narrator like *Sex and the City*'s Carrie Bradshaw. Based on the author of the book *Sex and the City* by Candace Bushnell, Carrie simply cannot shut up with all the narrating of herself and her friends' lives. Lots of us narrate things in our heads, but we don't subject millions of viewers to the running commentary (*paying* viewers, no less, until the show migrated to basic cable, where it makes up in ubiquity what it now lacks in priciness). And Carrie serves as a caution to all: writers can be dangerous to hang out with. That's because the quieter they're being on the outside, the more the little voice inside their head refuses to shut up. And since that little voice is the one that writes the syndicated newspaper column, you should watch what you say and do around it.

Carrie's life also teaches us that the myth of the rich writer is just that. Sure, Carrie lives in a Manhattan apartment big enough to hold a million Manolo Blahniks, but every once in a while you get the sense that her income isn't unlimited. That's probably because she's not exactly a superstar. She has problems with her agent and her editors and her publishers, and her book tour trip was rather a cheap affair. There are only so many Tom Clancys and Stephen Kings and John Grishams out there (one of each, in fact, by my unofficial count), and a lot more writers in the middle who have to struggle sometimes in order to continue affording an unlimited number of horrible outfits. In short, don't expect to be rich just because you're a published author or syndicated columnist. Unless you were rich before you started, in which case you'll probably be okay.

BUY, BUY, BUY

The most important thing to keep in mind about most mass media is that without advertising, a lot of it wouldn't exist. That's where the money comes from, whether you're in TV, radio, newspapers, or magazines. It's what finances the actors, the car crashes, the special effects, and the fact that in most cases people on TV only live their lives in eight- to ten-minute chunks. So advertising should get plenty of love and attention from TV characters, right?

Well, that's actually only half true. Back in the eighties, *thirtysomething* showed us that it was possible to be in advertising and still have a conscience. Michael and Elliot ran their own advertising firm, and were fairly successful without having to sell their souls right out of the gate. That came later.

After a few seasons, moneyman Miles Drentell swooped in. He wore nice suits, spoke literately, possessed smoothness and leadership ability in spades, and was generous with the financing. That's how we knew he was totally evil. After he'd been around for a while, Michael became so consumed with avoiding a takeover by Miles that he couldn't possibly have been doing anything else at work, like, say, making ads. Eventually Michael found himself overseeing an ad campaign for a political candidate whose ideas he had always disagreed with, but rationalized it to himself by changing some of his own. Unfortunately, this story line left us with a fairly large gap in the data; we knew Michael had sold his soul, but we never found out how much it went for. I'm not saying that I still own mine free and clear, mind you, but it would be nice to at least know how much equity I have in it.

If you're not too worried about your own soul, or never had one, you'd probably be happy at a place like the advertising agency on *Melrose Place*. Under the iron fist of Amanda Woodward, no tactic was too cold or self-serving. Certainly the firm couldn't have succeeded merely on the strength of its ideas because every time we saw someone doing a pitch, it was for some ridiculously stupid concept. Although it's also possible that the firm simply took care to select only clients who were even less advertising savvy than they were.

So clearly, TV writers must have some kind of love-hate relationship with the advertisers and advertising creatives who pay their bills. And it must make the writers even crazier in the modern era of product placement, where characters are expected to always hold their food and beverages so that the labels are clearly visible. NBC's *The Office* has taken in-show product placement further than anything that's been seen since the days of *Burns & Allen*, with characters constantly dropping whatever they're doing to extol the virtues of Staples or Benihana or Sandals. But even this strategy can seem rather backhanded. Yes, Michael

Scott is always happy to go on about how great these places are, but the fact that it's Michael Scott saying it is arguably a negative, since he's kind of an idiot. He can tell us how much he loves Chili's until he's blue in the face, but who in the viewing audience would be willing to take a chance on actually running into him there?

CONCLUSION

Getting involved in a workplace-based TV show on a regular basis is actually a lot like having a job. If you want to do it right, you have to show up at a regular time and stick around until it's done, but nobody will notice if your mind wanders once in a while in the meantime.

And how does working in the mass media compare to being a part of the workforce in general? Well, if there's anything that television teaches us, it's this: it's not as hard as you think. People in the biz succeed young, and they succeed big, often despite themselves. In addition to youthful Mary Richards, Dave Nelson didn't look a day over thirty when he started his job as the WNYX news director on *NewsRadio*, and even five years of working with those crazies didn't seem to age him much. Mass media is a young people's game, at almost every level of the organization. But that's okay, because based on the ages of most people in other lines of work on TV, so is almost everything else.

One difference: it's generally easier to quit watching a TV show than it is to quit your job. Less expensive, too, especially if the show in question is on HBO.

Learning Experiences

1 Write down a list of the five most out-of-line examples of workplace behavior you see on a given evening of channel surfing. Next day at work, imitate all of them. If you would prefer not to get fired, accuse someone else of having imitated all of them.

2 Count the number of total weirdos in your offices. If they all seem like weirdos to you, that can only mean that you're the weirdo.

3 Date someone in your office. If they're married, engaged, or in a serious relationship, wait until that's over. If *you're* married, engaged, or in a serious relationship, it was probably already over the moment you decided you were going to attempt this exercise.

4 Think about the longest day you've worked in the past year. Now think about the shortest day you've worked in the past year. If they are the same, your job is either too demanding or not demanding enough. Ask your spouse what he or she thinks. If you can't find your spouse, it's probably the former.

5 If you're not already in New York City, fly there. Then take a cab from JFK Airport to 30 Rock. Then fly to Los Angeles and take a cab from LAX to Studio 60 on the Sunset Strip. Time both cab trips to see which one is longer.

6 Poll media executives in your area to find out how old they are. You may be surprised to discover that they're not much older than the bosses on TV. Then do a little independent research to find out how old they really are.

7 Run a TV or radio station, magazine, newspaper, or advertising agency. Oh, it's not that hard. Quit your whining.

6

I'm No Superman

TV Medicine

It seems like there have been TV shows about doctors as long as there has been TV, if not as long as there have been doctors. In the old days, we had *Dr. Kildare* and *Ben Casey*. Now we have *Grey's Anatomy* and *House*. And *ER* just about bridges the gap between the two eras.

So why are there so many doctor shows? Why aren't there shows about patients? Aren't they the ones with the real problems?

Well, obviously not. Because no matter how badly off you might think you are when you show up in the emergency room after an accident that left your torso impaled by a giant brain tumor (and did I also mention that you're pregnant?), it's really all about the doctors.

If you get some exotic disease or spectacular injury

(and, as we know from television, they're always exotic and/or spectacular), you just know you're going to find yourself in the care of some sad-sack sawbones for whom your life-threatening condition is nothing more than a thematic reflection of whatever overwrought trauma is going on in his or her personal life this week.

I remember the last time I ended up in the emergency room. I had gone to my wife to tell her I had an awful headache, but my words came out as "Vacuum frog the of candlestick Spider-Man." I thought I had lost the use of words forever, a terrifying prospect for a writer.

But an ambulance ride and a CAT scan later, it turned out that I was just having a severe migraine that temporarily scrambled my brain's speech centers. With a good night's rest and a little more perspective, I was able to recognize the true purpose of my ailment: it was to help my doctor. I'm sure he'd been spending his shift confiding in a fellow medical professional about how much trouble he was having communicating with that special person in his life. And then I show up in the ER, barely able to force out a simple greeting like "Zipper for amaretto Tolstoy in ever crankshaft," and he realizes that saying what's in your mind and heart actually isn't that hard after all. Then he goes home, tells that special person how he really feels, and they fall into bed just as the credits roll. Glad to be of service, Doc. And thanks for that Imitrex prescription.

PROCEDURES

Never take a CPR class if you can help it. It'll only confuse you.

We all know how to do CPR from watching TV, right? Except that in CPR classes, they claim that doctors and lifeguards always get it wrong on TV. They do it with their hands out in front of them, rhythmically pressing on the victim's sternum lightly enough to not even get out of breath. But then the Red Cross tells you that you have to have your arms straight down under you, resting the weight of your entire upper body on the victim's chest and using only the heel of your hands, while you fling the force of your head and shoulders into the victim's chest cavity with each compression. Which sounds really painful for the victim, not to mention tiring for you. And then they tell you not to actually do that to your classmates upon whom you're practicing, and when you ask why it's done differently on TV, they say it's because if you do it correctly, you'll break the person's ribs. And this is the *right* way to do it?

The actual process of CPR isn't the only thing they teach you wrong. The last CPR class I took, they also "showed" us how to use a portable defibrillator. I figured I'd ace this, because I've seen it done a million times.

Step one: Squeeze a dollop of conductor gel on the paddles and rub them together. Refrain from making the obvious crack about whether the gel contains real conductors, at least until later.

Step two: Apply the paddles to the victim's chest.

Step three: Wait until that neato charging-up noise that sounds like a camera flash gets really high-pitched.

Step four: Yell, "Clear!"

Step five: Kick the table that the victim is lying on, hard enough to make him jerk up into the air. Repeat steps two through five, getting more and more upset each time, until the nurses start glancing nervously at one another.

Step six: Check to see if the victim has a pulse. This is easy to determine, because an electrocardiogram (or EKG for short, because TV doctors only talk and never have to spell or write anything and thus don't know that "electrocardiogram" doesn't have a *K* in it) will beep in rhythm with a pulse, and emit a piercing tone if the patient's heart is experiencing what's called a "flat line." But look at the EKG's monitor screen just to be sure. Look as desperate as possible.

Step seven: If the victim has a pulse, go limp with relief and walk out of the room, leaving less qualified professionals to handle the wrap-up. Skip any remaining steps. Are you wondering what to do if you get a pulse before this point? Don't. That never, ever happens. If there is still no pulse, proceed to step eight.

Step eight: Collapse, exhausted and grief-stricken, across the victim's chest, begging things like "Don't leave me!" or "It's not your time!" or "I never told you how I felt!" Remain in this position until a) you get a pulse, or b) some heartless prick announces to the room the exact time. In case of b), riding out of the room with the corpse on the gurney is optional, but it's probably a bit much.

Alas, portable defibrillators have taken all the fun out. It turns out they have these self-adhesive electrodes that you stick to the person, and then you press a red button on a little box. Sure, it saves lives and all, but in bringing defibrillation to the masses, they took the most dramatic thing you can do in a trauma room, and then they combined the thrill of a remote control and the excitement of Post-its.

And then there's blood transfusions. They sure sound cool, but on TV there's really not much to them; just a bag of blood hanging from an IV stand, looking gross. Medical science could really do TV a favor if it could figure out a way to do transfusions in a more dynamic fashion, preferably in a way that involved a fire hose. Just try to change the channel on that. TV also taught me that doctors were doing transfusions before they understood that there are different blood types, as on one occasion when Dr. Quinn, Medicine Woman, admitted to another character that nobody knew why blood transfusions didn't work sometimes. And with that sentence, I have officially made full use of every second of *Dr. Quinn, Medicine Woman* I have ever watched in my entire life.

Everyone has been present for at least one major medical procedure: childbirth.[1] But of course, doctors can't always be around for those, simply because labor is apparently only about a twenty-minute process, and is much more likely to happen in the back of a cab (as on an episode of *Taxi*), on an elevator stranded between floors (as on an episode of *7th Heaven*), or in Regis Philbin's lap (as on an episode of *Who Wants to Be a Millionaire?*).[2]

Not to worry. There are only a few things you really need. One of them is towels or hot water. And you can probably do without these. You can not, however, do without a completely freaked-out expression, and the English words *breathe* and *push*. Something that always happens on TV, but that nobody is ever prepared for, is that at some point in labor the mother will either threaten you with or commit upon your person some form of

---

1. You may deny ever having been at a childbirth. I would respond by asking how you got here, then.

2. This did not actually happen. But wouldn't it be great TV?

physical violence. For this reason you should also have a Taser gun ready so you can subdue her.[3]

Basically, there shouldn't be anything to worry about; the hardest thing you're likely to have to do, if the baby starts coming out ass- or feet-first, is to push it back in, turn it around inside the mother's womb, and tell her to start over. This is something you may want to practice with a pregnant woman before you need to actually do it, although keep in mind that approaching one on the street to make this request will require a considerable amount of tact. Work your way up to this by asking nonpregnant women first, as they are not nearly as moody.

But even this is probably unnecessary, as the most inopportune locations always result in a successful delivery. In fact, if you or your significant other is expecting, it may be to your advantage to choose not to give birth in a hospital or at home in the presence of a midwife, but in the front car of a roller coaster or the twentieth floor of a burning apartment building. Everything is going to go fine for you. Unless of course you are in fact a doctor who does this all the time, in which case see the bit about Dr. Greene from *ER* that's coming up a couple of pages from now and consider changing professions.

Long story short: if someone you love is experiencing some kind of medical trauma, the best thing to do is probably to put them in front of the TV.[4] That'll cure anything.

---

3. Under no circumstances should you use the Taser gun on the child after its birth, no matter how loudly it may be crying. Also, I would advise against attempting to use the Taser gun's electrical arc to cut the umbilical cord, as the stench will be unbearable.

4. Don't actually do this.

MEDICAL HISTORY

Early TV doctors like Ben Casey and Dr. Kildare (of the shows *Dr. Kildare* and *Ben Casey*—not necessarily in that order) were such noble heroes, always putting their patients ahead of other concerns, such as getting a little poontang. That's because back in the olden days, people had a lot more respect for authority and its institutions, like the medical profession.

But then the Kennedy assassinations and the Vietnam war put an end to all of that, and TV responded less than a decade later with the first antiwar medical show, *M*A*S*H*. A wacky group of combat surgeons, some of whom served during all eleven years of the three-year Korean War, traded wisecracks while elbow-deep in shrapnel and viscera. We learned that doctors can be nutty and irreverent—at least the good ones. Frank Burns, for example, didn't enjoy a good joke, and you certainly didn't want that guy rooting around in your thorax. Just leave the shrapnel where it is, if it's all the same to you.

Not that the war didn't leave some pretty hideous scars on those kooky doctors. I'm not sure Alan Alda was ever funny again; *Trapper John, M.D.* fetched up in the eighties as a bald guy who, if he'd gotten into the laughing gas, might occasionally approach a slightly droll mood; and don't even get me started on *After M*A*S*H* (at least not until Chapter 13). Moral: The operating room is a tough place to stay funny.[5]

---

5. M*A*S*H is also where I learned about the army chain of command and what each rank of officer does. Generals are far away. Colonels and lieutenant colonels are in charge, majors are pompous assholes, captains are fun to be around, and lieutenants are nurses. For sergeants and privates you have to go to *Gomer Pyle, U.S.M.C.*

Nowhere is that more clear than on *St. Elsewhere*. Yes, that show's most memorable single image is probably that of Dr. Craig head-butting Dr. Ehrlich over a surgical patient's cracked chest. But man, was that show a downer. Ever get the idea that hospitals are gleaming cathedrals of science and healing and hot doctors? The medical hellhole called St. Eligius will straighten you out on that a lot faster than it could ever straighten out your tib-fib fracture.[6] An hour watching *St. Elsewhere* is an hour in a place with not enough funds, too many deaths, and a staff of doctors who actually look like doctors as opposed to models. Notable exceptions to the charisma-challenged staff of this otherwise hottie-free hospital included Denzel Washington, who now wins Oscars; Howie Mandel, who now tells dozens of models which briefcases to open on a game show; and Mark Harmon, whose character had the dubious distinction of being the first network series regular to die of AIDS (more cheeriness!). But they were more than counterbalanced by clock stoppers like David Morse, Ed Flanders, and Ed Begley Jr. Nobody called those guys Dr. Mc-Dreamy. And their lives weren't any easier on our hearts than their faces were on our eyes. From *St. Elsewhere,* we learned the reassuring lesson that doctors were just as miserable and emotionally fucked up as the rest of us; they just know longer words and have worse handwriting. Or at least they do in the imagination of an autistic child sparked by gazing into a snow globe, which is what the whole series turned out to be anyway. Not to put down those who live with autism in real life, but thanks for pulling the stakes right out from under yourself at the end there, *St. E.*

---

6. The X-rays for which will either a) reveal a previously unknown tumor, or b) give you one.

Then in 1994, what was supposed to be a groundbreaking medical show premiered, with a regular time slot on Thursday nights at ten Eastern. If someone had told you back then that this hospital-based drama would end up as a network flagship series, lasting over a dozen seasons until its entire original cast was gone and yet was still going strong, you would have thought they were crazy. And since that show was CBS's *Chicago Hope*, you would have been right.

Meanwhile, in the same time slot but over on another network, NBC had figured out a way to combine the breakneck pace of the 4077th with the heartbreaking angst of *St. Elsewhere*, and then double both. The result was *ER*. We all learned a valuable lesson from this show, and we learned it quick. In the late eighties and early nineties, everyone I knew was complaining about how long you had to wait every time you went to the emergency room with the flu or an infected zit or whatever. Then *ER* premiered and we quickly got to see why: it's because doctors and nurses are too busy swarming around victims of car and subway accidents who make the grenade- and bullet-shredded patients on *M*A*S*H* look like . . . well, like people with the flu and infected zits. And that's *before* the paramedics start slamming their gurneys laden with yet more grisly products of the latest traffic holocaust through those incredibly noisy double doors. Emergency-room people don't have time for me and you, because as soon as they're done flailing and tubing and jargoning and statting around one poor maimed bastard, another one (or fifty) is on the way. Not to mention how hard it must be dodging the Steadicams that are swooping all over the place. Everyone I know watched *ER* the first few seasons. And they quit complaining about how long they had to wait in the emergency room themselves.[7]

That's because *ER* showed us that hospital emergency rooms aren't just inconvenient; they're downright dangerous. Let's say it's March 1995 and you land at County General with a minor pregnancy issue. You meet your doctor, a gentleman named Mark Greene. You and he and your husband get along great at first. An hour later, for no good reason, you're dead. Trust me, after that you're going to have a few choice words for Dr. Greene when he shows up seven years later at the Pearly Gates courtesy of brain cancer. Some of those words might even be, "So how long's that tumor been in there, anyway?"

Or maybe you'll be lucky enough to meet one of Dr. Greene's colleagues, Doug Ross, in a more social setting. You have a few drinks, go home with him, have a little anonymous sex, do some drugs in his bathroom. Next morning, you're dead.[8] Beats watching him in *Batman and Robin,* but not by much.

But don't bet on encountering any particular doctor because they keep leaving. Since we first met them in 1994, County General has seen the departure of every original main cast member. While the same secondary characters like nurses and desk people stuck around for over a decade, avoiding burnout by never having too many lines, the original first-stringers have long since been replaced by the likes of Corday, Kovic, Romano, Pratt, Gal-

---

7. The other important thing we learned is how dangerous it is to be a commuter in the Chicagoland area. Between all the multicar pileups on the Kennedy Expressway, crashes on the El, and rescue helicopters constantly falling from the sky, it's a wonder any Chicagoans ever got to work at all.

8. Maybe it's worth it for a night with George Clooney. I'm not one to judge.

lant, Chen, Lockhart, Rasgotra, Gardner, Ericson, and Tripp. And even I'm not sure which of those names I just made up.

If you can't hack the kind of pace and pathos served up by *ER* (not to mention the dizzying staff turnover), make sure you end up at a hospital like the one on *Scrubs,* where you'll find yourself around the wisecracking J. D., Turk, and the other goofs at Sacred Heart who not only aren't buried in blood in the ER's front lines, but have nothing but time to sit around in the cafeteria making jokes and indulging in frequent five-second fantasy sequences. More importantly, these young interns represent the next logical step in the evolution of the TV doctor. If *M*A*S*H* made doctors fun, and *St. Elsewhere* and *ER* made them flawed, *Scrubs* made them more relatable than ever by showing us that doctors can also be losers and dorks. Now, *that's* comforting.

Fortunately, TV shows us even more options. In the 2004– 2005 season, two hit medical dramas premiered featuring memorable male leads: one McDreamy, and one McPissy.

No bedside manner? No love life? No people skills at all? Dr. Greg House, the protagonist of *House,* is, we are told, a brilliant diagnostician. So brilliant, in fact, that when somebody shows up at his hospital with lungs turning to stone or a skull flipping itself inside out, he is able to diagnose the problem not only once, but two or three times per episode. He's also a gimpy Vicodin addict who hates everyone. Clearly, this is not a man who chose his profession to "help people." Sure, he's a genius, but his encyclopedic knowledge of every imaginable ailment is trumped by one vital tenet of his medical philosophy: patients always lie. This is followed closely by its corollary, which is that patients' families always lie. This one comes into play more often than one might think, primarily when the treatment for the first diagnosis exacerbates the problem, sending the patient into a coma from which he or she cannot lie for him or herself.

House's other diagnostic crutch (if you'll pardon the expression) is the fact that he believes every other doctor on the show is an idiot who is always wrong. As with his other belief, he is usually correct.

But aside from these factors, House decides on a course of treatment by asking himself a series of questions, just like any other doctor. These questions are:

1. How is the patient lying to me?
2. How is the patient's family lying to me?
3. What do the other doctors think? Because the opposite is probably true.
4. Where's my Vicodin?

And so lives are saved. See? Being a doctor is easy!

The only doctors less focused on you the patient (and more on themselves) than the doctors at Sacred Heart and the doctors at Princeton-Plainsboro Teaching Hospital are the doctors at Seattle Grace on *Grey's Anatomy*. Even the title sequence of *Grey's* is straightforward about its mission as a medical/romantic show, with clinical images melding and juxtaposing themselves with visuals associated with romance and dating. For instance, there's the IV bag that morphs into a martini glass, the scalpel that becomes a lipstick, the open-chested cadaver on the autopsy table that is replaced by a steaming lasagna (I may be imagining that last one).

And the imagery is more than lived up to by the actual show and its characters. Those people switch partners more often than square dancers. They of all people, with their medical knowledge and awareness of how diseases are spread, should know that when you sleep with one person, you're sleeping with all their previous sexual partners. By this logic, I suspect that at this point half of the cast has slept with me, and the other half has slept with you. There may even be some overlap, but I don't want to seem too forward with you. I started to put together a little diagram outlining who all has slept with whom, but it quickly started to look like an M. C. Escher drawing and I could feel this headache coming on and the last thing I need is another speech-scrambling migraine to make me saltine bone this yellow at retainer.

Aside from knowing that your doctors will be way too distracted by one another to focus on you, you also want to beware of boring them with your broken leg. Ordinary ailments need not apply. In fact, the characters have even come to expect a certain degree of surgical weirdness in their daily lives. A sample exchange from season three:

Chief: There was a *fish* in a man's *penis.*
Dr. Bailey (scoffing): There will *always* be a fish in a man's penis.

You want to really surprise these characters? Give them a day when there's nothing to do but simple bypasses and angioplasties.[9] It'll blow their minds.

---

9. At least they're safe from having to treat lacerations from broken glass. As should be readily apparent to anyone who watches TV, crashing bodily through a plate-glass window or having a bottle smashed over your head is cause for no more than a momentary inconvenience, and certainly doesn't merit a hospital stay.

Basically, unless you're a pregnant man or you have an unexploded bomb in your abdomen, you're not likely to get much attention. That's because your doctors are busy doing one of two things: trying to get in on the more exotic cases (as if another five or six equally bizarre victims aren't going to be coming in later today) or keeping track of who is having sex with whom. At the nominal center of all this hoo-ha is protagonist Meredith Grey, a surgical intern who can't ever seem to get her personal shit together yet insists on lecturing us with some meaningless voice-over narration at the beginning and end of nearly every episode. There's another ABC show with an annoying narrator: *Desperate Housewives*, for which our guide is the late Mary Alice Young. Unlike Mary Alice, Meredith is, as of this writing, not dead. She's come close a couple of times, but it turned out she was only teasing.

CONCLUSION

So this is the state of modern medicine? Assholes, nerds, self-absorbed sex maniacs, and people who can't help but narrate their own lives?

One wonders what kind of doctors the future holds. Idiots who don't know a central line from a Pap smear? Sociopaths who kill their patients on purpose? The return of naive idealists like Dr. Kildare and Ben Casey, who in the modern world will only end up getting eaten alive by the insurance companies and malpractice lawyers? Thank God it's the nurses who actually seem to run these places.

Physicians, heal thyselves. And don't come near us until you do.

Learning Experiences

1 Take a CPR certification course from your local American Red Cross chapter. Be sure to tell everyone else in the class whenever the instructor tries to tell you something that's wrong.

2 Impersonate a doctor. Just to be safe, you should probably avoid doing this activity in a hospital or clinic. Much safer to do it in a movie theater, during church, or in the privacy of your own home. If an actual medical emergency arises, skip out immediately.

3 At your next doctor's appointment, quiz your physician in great detail about his or her sexual history and that of his or her colleagues.

4 Beware the simple diagnosis. If your doctor seems to figure out what's wrong with you right away, you're doomed to be misdiagnosed at least two more times within the hour. But don't worry; it may seem impossible, but you'll always pull through. Unless it's during sweeps, when your doctor is gunning for an Emmy and the chance to show "range." Then you are, to use a medical term, toast.

7

Don't Do the Crime
If You Can't Do the Time

Law Enforcement and Crime Solving

You've heard of "The Academy," right? Not the people who give out the Oscars, but that place where they teach cops to be cops? In fact, you probably first heard of it on a cop show. Maybe you've even seen a film or two that was set there. Of course those *Police Academy* movies are wildly inaccurate; if those kind of wacky, R-rated high jinks were really that commonplace, would the institution really accept a little girl, let alone three of them, as the introduction to *Charlie's Angels* clearly states it did once upon a time?

In any case, training people is time-consuming and expensive in any profession, let alone one where the trainees can accidentally shoot one another. It would be much more cost-effective to sit would-be crime fighters down and have them watch police shows for a year or so. Then they could learn what they really need to know to make it on the street. Or better yet, just read this chapter, buy a gun, and get out there.[1] Think of this as your own personal Police Academy. It's quick, it's convenient, and best of all, there's no Steve Guttenberg.

THE COP'S LIFE CYCLE

The most important thing to do in your first year on the force is watch and learn. Inevitably, you'll be partnered with a crusty old veteran who's just seconds from retirement, and he (never she) will have a lot to teach you. But will you listen to him, or to the seasoned lieutenant who keeps complaining to you about all the heat he (or she) keeps getting from both upstairs and downtown? Of course you won't. You'll insist on continuing to do things your own stubborn, impulsive, hot-tempered way. Not that it matters; only one of you is likely to die, and if you both make it through the pilot, your chances of survival go up considerably.

Still, once you get past that point, you can't take things for granted. Make sure your holster is nice and accessible because whatever real cops tell you about how they go months and sometimes years without ever drawing their weapons in the line of duty? Someone must be misleading us because cops on TV point their guns at people several times an hour. Some of them draw so often that they're probably in danger of sustaining re-

---

1. Don't actually do this.

petitive motion injuries. With gunplay occurring that frequently in the line of duty, it doesn't pay to be unprepared.

Look what happened to poor Tim Speedle on *CSI: Miami*, who ignored this advice. In the middle of a pitched shoot-out, he was staring down the barrel of a bad guy's gun when his own weapon jammed. Speedle survived by dumb luck, received a gun-cleaning kit afterward as a pointed "gift" from his asshole boss Horatio Caine, and then got killed for real the next time his gun jammed. The force is no place for slobs (okay, I'll grant you Columbo; but it's not like he was all about gunfights).

Eventually, though, you won't be the newest recruit on the force anymore. Someone younger and greener always comes along. Don't make friends with them. They'll be dying soon.

As your years on "the job" (everyone calls it "the job," which almost implies that no other profession is a job at all, which would explain why they're always willing to interrupt people at work) tick past, you'll eventually reach the midpoint of your career. You have two ways to go from here. You can be the competent, heroic, yet world-weary man of action, or you can be the regular-guy-type secondary character who provides comic relief (your Medavoys from *NYPD Blue*, your Switeks from *Miami Vice*). The latter strikes me as a lot more restful, but you're of course free to make your own decisions.

There's an old saying that goes, "There are old soldiers and bold soldiers, but there are no old, bold soldiers." The same can't be said of cops. Police detectives on TV don't get any less brave as their years of service pile up. In fact, they're often prepared to sacrifice themselves in order to spare a younger cop. Such courage never goes unrewarded; the more willing an aging officer is to go to that big station house in the sky, the more spectacular the deus ex machina that will save his life.

And look at that, you made it. Now all you need to do is hold on until retirement, which at this point is only seconds away. But, oops—the chief just partnered you with a green new recruit, asking you to show him the ropes. And things are going to get interesting all over again. Sucks to be you.

INVESTIGATIVE TECHNIQUES

In any murder investigation, you build a case with three pillars. The first is motive: Why was the murder committed? The second is opportunity: Could a suspect have committed the murder? If your suspect was already dead or in jail at the time, probably not. The third is either a weapon or a body. I can't remember which. That's because television is a dynamic medium, and not so much with the static visual aids that would help me retain things like this. Similarly, my plan is to just keep moving too quickly to give you time to reflect on my ignorance in this area. Oh, I think another pillar is cause of death, and also the fact that if you have a highly recognizable special guest star on your mystery show, that's the one who did it. Okay, that's enough pillars. We still need to leave ourselves room to walk around and take lots of photos, after all.

We're told that the majority of murder cases in real life go unsolved. This is a difficult concept to get our brains around. Not just because it means that the majority of murderers are still wandering around out there, but because we don't know what an unsolved case looks like. Unless Robert Stack or John Walsh is on hand, you never see detectives on TV investigating a murder for an hour, and then at the end turning to the camera and saying, "Well, we didn't solve this one. Sorry about that. See you next week!" Audiences would say, "Uh, no, you won't."

Real-life cops will try to claim that this is because viewers want a story with a beginning, a middle, and an end when they sit down to watch TV (the relatively recent success of prime-time serial mysteries like *24* and *Lost* notwithstanding). But I suspect that's only because they don't want to deal with the high expectations that TV investigations set for them. I mean, if you're a TV cop and don't find the bad guy in an hour, you're probably not going to find him at all. From *Law & Order* to *Homicide: Life on the Street* to *The X-Files* to most of the several dozen other shows on which Richard Belzer has played Detective John Munch, the whole point is to get someone put away.

The two exceptions to this rule are the "recurring nemesis" clause, which we'll get to in a minute, and the other one is the cold case, without which we wouldn't have *Cold Case*. Each week on that show, Detective Lily Rush and her merry band of mystery exhumers manage to find some puzzler that somehow slipped through the cracks of other detective shows from the nineties all the way back to before TV itself. The *Cold Case* team has at its disposal powerful tools their predecessors didn't have: high technology, DNA analysis, the Patriot Act. Too bad they don't use any of these.

They're clearly unnecessary, anyway, because all you apparently need is an hour of questionable testimony (and even more questionable period outfits, hairstyles, and background music) to close in on the guilty killer who's gone free lo these many decades.[2] But take heart, because people who can't seem to retain simple things will be able to recall seemingly insignificant clues decades down the road, so that the victims' families can finally have the satisfaction of knowing the killer will be behind bars for the last several weeks of his or her life.

So obviously, the only way to avoid prosecution indefinitely is to find a cop-show protagonist and become his or her recurring nemesis (as per the "recurring-nemesis clause" mentioned above). Watching *Law & Order: Criminal Intent*, you may wonder how anybody in New York City ever gets away with anything. Lead detective Robert Goren has an eerie gift for getting inside suspects' heads. And once he's there, he commences kicking over anything he can find. Almost invariably, the final scene of each episode features Goren and several other people confronting the killer, lulling him into a false sense of security, then trapping him into a confession. If you too can stage these little theater pieces in which everyone knows his or her role except the killer (even the killer's defense attorney, who will somehow always know that his or her job is to keep his or her trap shut while you blatantly harass his or her client), you will not only get to show your brilliance, but, like Goren, you will always get your man.

Your woman, however, is a different story. At least four times now, Goren has come up against his opposite number. Unlike

---

2. In the process, they're forced to rely on the memories of people who don't even remember what the other suspects looked like at the time of the murder. For instance, in one recent episode, an aged suspect was played by Robert Pine, probably best remembered as Sarge from the seventies biker-cop borderline-porn series *CHiPs*. A younger version of Pine's character was being played in flashbacks by a different actor. The problem is that we the viewers remember what Pine looked like thirty years ago, and it was nothing like Dale the Weasel from *ER*, who played Pine's younger self.

him, she's a hot blonde,[3] but they share a similar twisted genius for understanding crime. She, of course, uses hers for evil, and to escape the clutches of the law . . . until next time.

The same holds true on *CSI: Crime Scene Investigations* (the original). In most cases, a combination of cutting-edge science, dogged detective work, and witty banter—all supported by a NASA-size budget, judging by the look of that Las Vegas crime lab—will find the truth just in time for the closing credits. Except when they don't. Fortunately, those who would otherwise get away with their crimes always commit more, and it's only a matter of time until they slip. In the first season, a killer named Paul Millander killed, skated, and then killed again, which is what got him pinched. In a more recent season, the crime-lab crew was plagued by a serial murderer who not only had time to commit the crimes and rid the scenes of all damning evidence, but also went to the trouble of building the investigators miniature models of each crime scene. If Martha Stewart became a serial killer, this is how she would go about it.

But sooner or later, everyone gets caught. Even if you have to wait until the season finale to see it happen. Even Dr. Kimble finally caught up with the murderous one-armed man in the final episode of *The Fugitive* back in 1967. Don't tell me what happened, though; I still haven't gotten around to watching it on my TiVo.

So how do all these cases get sewn up? There are a number of important steps to follow and pitfalls to look out for.

The most important skill to develop is interviewing suspects

---

3. Who would have thought that Kevin Arnold's hippie older sister from *The Wonder Years* would ditch David Schwimmer to become a criminal mastermind?

and witnesses. They're not always going to be especially committed to helping you, even if they're innocent. It seems like you always catch them at work or in a hurry to somewhere important, and they're so impatient to get back to their lives that generally they're the ones who end the interview. Unless you have them in an interrogation room at the station house, there isn't much you can do about this, so be sure to get the information you need quickly. If it takes you more than forty-five seconds to glean a relevant fact that either advances your investigation or proves someone lied to you earlier, you're doing it wrong.

Every investigator has to be prepared for the big question that comes up at least once per investigation. At some point, someone—whether it be a suspect, a suspect's friend, or just a witness—will utter some variation of the gambit "That's not a crime, is it?" There are a number of possible responses to this roadblock, and the one you use is dependent on the circumstances. Favorites are as follows:

1. "No, but murder is." Advantages: always applies, is never not true, quite pithy. Disadvantages: not all that imaginative. Therefore it gets used more than any response.

2. "Actually, it is." Advantages: throws the suspect for a loop, putting them at a disadvantage. Also lets you know you're dealing with an idiot, if the supposedly noncriminal activity consists of lying to police, interfering with a crime scene, or, in rare cases, actual murder. Disadvantages: You have to keep track of what's actually illegal and what isn't, which is more of a law-

yer's job. Also, a confession of, say, littering may not provide the leverage you expect it to.

3. "No, but your significant other/employer/parents might think so." Advantages: works well on people who have a secret to keep. Disadvantages: makes you a blackmailer, only works on people with secrets to keep. The good news is that depending on how "dark" this investigation is, everyone will have a secret to keep.

4. "No. Thanks for your time." Advantages: ends the interview quickly. Disadvantages: gets you nowhere.

Other important investigative tools include rubber gloves to wear at the crime scene, a mordantly convivial relationship with the local medical examiner, and of course the well-timed wisecrack. Lennie Briscoe on the original *Law & Order* had such remarkable facility with this item that for a while, TNT replayed one back during every rerun. This was a shrewd move because as every human being alive has seen every Briscoe-era episode of *Law & Order* several times, the only remaining mystery was which of Briscoe's many quips would be selected for inclusion during the halftime break.

But any TV detective worth his badge knows that the most important tool in his arsenal is the clock. If it's ten minutes before the hour, you know a confession is imminent and it's time to ramp up the intensity of interrogation. If it's twenty minutes before the hour and your investigation has hit a dead end, worry not; a clue is about to drop into your lap that will lead you to where you'll need to be in ten minutes. And when you do get a confession, check the time. If it's less than five minutes before the hour, you're golden. If it's only half past, you now have two mysteries on your hands: the actual murder, and the question of why the person confessing to the crime is lying to you.

One thing you need to look out for: the better the show you're on (or the more ambitious its pretensions), the greater the frequency with which guilty people will walk away. I'm not talking about unsolved murders. I'm talking about crimes where you know who did it, and he knows you know he did it, yet he walks anyway thanks to some sleazy lawyer, obscure technicality, or his own diabolical cleverness. It sucks, but we all have to grow up sometime. All you can do in situations like this is hope for the best from the nemesis clause further down the road.

THE CUTTING EDGE

In recent decades, advances in modern science have introduced to armchair detectives three initials starting with *C* and ending with *I*, which strike fear into the hearts of the guilty and hope into the unjustly accused. In years past, the technology didn't exist to bring the facts of a crime into such indisputable, sharp relief. And it's all thanks to a simple trio of letters: *CGI*.

Short for "Computer Generated Image," CGI can now take us inside the lungs of a drowning victim, inside the blood of a poisoning victim, and inside the petechial hemorrhaging of a strangulation victim. And sometimes even into DNA. Most effectively (and most frequently) used at the aforementioned Las Vegas Crime Lab (and somewhat less so at its Miami and New York counterparts), CGI is the true master detective. And master teacher too. You and I aren't the only ones who have learned a great deal about forensic science in the light of its animated pixels; prosecutors and police across the country have complained about the *"CSI* effect," in which juries are demanding more conclusive forensic evidence before providing convictions. They say it's making it harder to put criminals in jail, but I suspect they're just like our parents, telling us to stop watching so much television for selfish and mysterious reasons of their own. I'd look into what those reasons are, but I can't afford any of my own CGI.

PRIVATE EYES

Private detectives just aren't what they used to be. By which I mean they're less numerous. In the seventies and eighties, you couldn't click from two to twelve (our only channels back then) without hitting a Jim Rockford, a Thomas Magnum, a (first name unknown) Spenser, a (first name and last name unknown) going by the name Remington Steele, or a pair of Simons. These days you have to actively seek out PI role models, and when you find one, they're all kind of damaged somehow. Michael Westen from *Burn Notice* only gumshoes because he's not allowed to be a spy anymore. Adrian Monk from *Monk* has so many phobias and hang-ups that the real mystery is how he ever manages to leave his apartment. Shawn Spencer from *Psych* has a photographic memory that he uses to trick people into thinking he's psychic. Worse yet, every single one of these shamuses (shami?) lives on USA instead of a real TV network.

This is a rare case where TV audiences picked up the opposite message that the people in the box were trying to convey. We were all supposed to believe that private eyes lived exciting lives in which they were constantly being beaten up and shot at in between seductions/betrayals by beautiful women. Yet somehow, word got out that real life wasn't living up to these standards. Far from continuing to believe that a private eye's life is an exciting one, people began to realize that a real-life detective's idea of an exciting evening is to spend the entire night in a parked car, peeing in a coffee can and waiting for a chance to take telephoto pictures of ugly people having sex they're not supposed to be having. Used to be they could also expect to spend a lot of time in the library or the newspaper morgue digging through stultifyingly dull records, but the advent of the Internet has made this pursuit largely unnecessary, not to mention even less TV-friendly. In short, the primary prerequisite for being a private detective seems to be a superhuman ability to stay awake. If there's a true-to-life depiction of a private eye's daily routine on the air right now, it's on at 3 a.m. and targeted at insomniacs.

On TV, however, an obvious but infrequently commented-upon trait that is required for any successful private investigator is the ability to attract crime. It's easy for some, like the Blue Moon Detective Agency on *Moonlighting* or Remington Steele, who can just paint a name on their door and wait for the crimes to come in. The disturbing thing is that it's also easy for people who *don't* do that and yet still manage to stumble upon a murder just about every day of their lives.

Exhibit A through Omega is Jessica Fletcher, the mystery novelist played by Angela Lansbury on the interminable CBS series *Murder, She Wrote*. Jessica lived in a small New England town (and later, New York), but had the insatiable wanderlust so common among biddies of means. She also killed more people than Hitler. Every week for twelve years, somebody would drop dead in close proximity to this woman. This shouldn't be surprising, since the demographic she ran with was certainly prone to the deadly scourges of strokes, heart attacks, and the dreaded "natural causes." And yet nobody could ever seem to wait for events to take their course; they just had to wipe out their victim right now, often for no other reason than that Jessica Fletcher was around to solve the mystery. Has anybody reading this been close to even one mysterious death or murder in their entire lives? Let alone several thousand? Maybe some seasoned homicide detectives have, but they probably stopped reading several pages ago in a huff. My theory is that all along, it was Angela herself orchestrating these murders, then framing her chosen "perps" and hypnotizing them into confessing when the time came (all of this activity would have taken place during commercial breaks, of course).

There were two mysteries I always wanted her to solve, though, even though I knew she never would. The first was how she found time to bang out a novel on her typewriter based on each case during the seven-day windows that separated them; and the second was why people kept inviting her over. It's not just that death followed her everywhere; it's also that I can't figure out how she still had any surviving friends by the third season.

ORDER IN THE COURT

Clarence Darrow said that anyone who represents himself in court has a fool for a client.[4] I even knew it when I went to court to defend myself, acting as my own advocate.

---

4. I learned that from a one-man show about Darrow starring Henry Fonda on PBS, so it counts.

Aside from that first fact, I didn't know much about courtrooms. *Perry Mason* reruns are no help, mind you; all I ever learned from those is that nobody ever objects to Perry's courtroom theatrics in the last few minutes once he gets up a good steam of inadmissible outrageousness. He can badger, harangue, and filibuster a witness and the prosecutor will just sit back and watch the show. I knew I couldn't count on this, especially with my lack of oratorical flair. It seemed much wiser to draw my legal lessons from a more reliable source, like *Law & Order*.

As everyone knows by now, *Law & Order* is the only show in which they spend the first half of every episode finding the perps and the second half trying to put them away.[5] What is it about the original that gives it such longevity? It's not the "chung-chung" scene transitions; it can't be the cast, which has been through a number of iterations higher than Sam Waterston's age. It's because a half hour is about as long as you really need to see a courtroom these days to pick up all you need to know. Even Matlock spent more of his time investigating in the real world than arguing in front of a jury.

Dick Wolf's genius was to find a way to put a half-hour courtroom drama into an hour of television. If you'd rather be a lawyer than a cop, just tune in to the last half hour of each of TNT's thirty-eight daily reruns for the next few years and hang up your shingle.

I exaggerate, of course. Being set in New York City, *Law & Order* tends to focus on local and state laws that might not be

---

5. Other shows may be called *Law & Order*, but they either concentrate on the cops (*Law & Order: Sex Police* and *Law & Order: Defense Attorneys Are for Suckers*) or disappear after a few episodes (*Law & Order: Trial by Jury* and *Conviction*, the latter of which ended up being so bad that executive producer Dick Wolf withheld the *Law & Order* designation and was probably tempted to do the same with his own name).

applicable in, say, Vancouver. So even watching it for years is no substitute for law school. Unless, of course, you live in New York.

TV shows focusing on the law also demonstrate how life threatening all that dull courtroom stuff can actually be. *Night Court* went the half-hour comedy route, but only for long enough to kill off half a dozen elderly bailiff-portraying actresses, and eventually the body count became too high to justify the human cost of keeping judges and lawyers on the network. At least until *L.A. Law* came along, and even that show had a tendency to drop people down elevator shafts.

One of the foundations of legal study, as we all know from those seasons of *The Paper Chase*, is the study of case law. Precedent rules all. That maxim is upheld every week on *Law & Order*, when attorneys are having some argument in judges' chambers and are always trumping one another by spouting off names of cases like *Plessy v. Ferguson* or *Brown v. Board of Education* or *People of New York v. Boston*. Except the cases they mention are ones that you and I have never heard of. For all I knew, they could have just been making up these cases on the spot to support their arguments, and the judge and opposing attorney would go along so as not to seem ignorant.

So then I broke my cardinal rule on this project, and dug a little deeper. I had noticed that the closing credits on *Law & Order* always mention something called WestLaw. Sometimes the attorneys even mention it onscreen. WestLaw turns out to be an online database of case law. It costs a bomb to access, though, and I'm not earning defense attorney money, so I turned to a lawyer friend of mine who said that all of the case names cited on *Law & Order* that she recognized actually seemed to support what the attorneys claimed. This is good for verisimilitude, but it's bad for someone who wants to be a lawyer without working at it.

So if you're really determined to pursue law as a career, it's going to be harder than you thought. Study case law. By which I mean, of course, watch the show religiously. Write down the names of these cases and what they're about, and at least you'll have an edge on people who haven't even bothered to do that. Oh, and those motions and briefs that people are always handing to one another? I'm pretty sure they're blank. When Jack McCoy was an ADA, everyone was always handing him a folded sheet of blue paper and identifying it as "motion to dismiss" or "motion to strike" some critical piece of evidence. And he never even opened them, let alone read them; he just stood there looking sad and defeated as though the motion had already been granted, and then ran to whoever his boss was that season to ask him or her what to do now. If a supposedly dedicated guy like McCoy could be so easily conned, imagine what a real lawyer would buy.

This might explain the disappointing conviction rate on *Law & Order*. Sure, most of the bad guys get put away, but that's because the case has already been solved by this point. The hard working, fast-quipping, lucky-as-hell detectives in the first half did their jobs (unless they didn't, in which case they're called to testify and then get yelled at by the lawyers for something they supposedly screwed up). Still, the most important aspect of a mystery's solution is whodunit, not whatnext. Thanks to the occasional technicality or extra-sneaky defense lawyering, sometimes a perp will walk. And then the only comfort our heroes have is a few dark wisecracks on their way to the elevator.

CONCLUSION

I only wish I knew all this when I went to court. At that time, I hadn't seen as much *Law & Order* as I have now, so pretty much all I was sure about is that you call a judge "Your Honor" and aren't allowed to make statements to a witness, only ask questions. Still, after my guilty verdict was read and the bailiff escorted me out of the courtroom, she assured me, "You were in it for a while, there." That's all the encouragement I needed. Next time I'll be ready, and traffic court won't know what hit it.

Learning Experiences

1 Invest in a police scanner and learn what all those number codes mean by going to the address provided by the dispatcher and finding out what's going on. Here's a head start: according to *CSI*, a "419" is generally not a load of laughs.

2 Pick a crime that occurred recently in your neighborhood. Conduct all investigation, interviews, arrests, prosecutions, and sentencings. If this task seems too daunting at first, try warming up by committing the crime yourself.

3 Reconstruct the recent movements of a family member, neighbor, roommate, or friend using the most advanced forensic techniques currently available. Before beginning, make sure you can secure financing for fingerprint powders, DNA testing equipment, ultraviolet lights, a gas chromatograph, and a full AV editing and enhancement suite.

4 Argue a case in court. If you just walk into your local courthouse, there's bound to be something going on. Feel free to par-

ticipate in oral arguments, witness examinations, what have you. But talk quickly, because you might not get to stay for very long.

5 Get a PI license. Be aware that this will require you to go through a great deal of paperwork, testing, and some form of life-altering trauma that leaves you with a number of eccentricities.

8

Moving On Up

Unreal Estate

Most people's shelter needs aren't that complicated. All they really need are three solid-appearing walls around them and a lighting grid over their heads.

If you still haven't moved out of your parents' place, what are you waiting for? Are you worried that you won't find a nice enough or big enough place? As we all know from watching TV, all places are nice enough and big enough—even the places that aren't supposed to be.

Maybe that's why so many homes look alike. We've all driven past subdivisions that look more like hives than communities, with row after row of identical structures. And according to TV, they don't look much different inside. Aliens who have been tuning in to American TV shows could probably build houses of their own just from seeing how many domestic interiors are almost exactly alike.

To start with, you've got your living room. The front door is on the right side of the TV screen. There's some kind of desk or credenza against the wall right next to it.[1] The sofa occupies pride of place in the middle of the room, with a few cushy chairs arranged here and there. The back wall is dominated by an open staircase that takes you to the left of the screen as you climb it. Opposite the front door is the entrance to the kitchen, which is separated from the living room by a swinging door. The kitchen has a table on the right, as well as a counter that employs a center island (or at least peninsula) configuration on the left. And opposite the door from the living room, there's another door that leads you to either the backyard or the garage. There are other rooms, but since you never see anyone leaving or entering them from the aforementioned two primary living spaces, they may as well be in another dimension.

Am I overgeneralizing? Of course. But just off the top of my head, the sitcom families that shared this same floor plan included the Huxtables (*The Cosby Show*), the Bunkers (*All in the Family*), the Drummonds (*Diff'rent Strokes*), the Sheffields (*The Nanny*), the Barones (*Everybody Loves Raymond*), the Westons (*Empty Nest*), the Taylors (*Home Improvement*), the Rushes (*Too Close for Comfort*), and the Keatons (*Family Ties*). Okay, *Family Ties* was a little different, but you know that departure was just the kind of stubborn parental Keatonian nonconformity that consistently drove Alex up a wall.

---

1. The desk or credenza will have one drawer, and that drawer will always contain only the specific item you need right now and nothing else. I need to get me one of those.

And there were occasional other variations. The Stevenses on *Bewitched*, the Conners on *Roseanne*, and the Petries on *The Dick Van Dyke Show* all entered their homes and their living rooms from the left side of the screen. But just like everyone else, once they got into the room (provided Rob Petrie didn't give himself a concussion just walking in), there was always a sofa facing nothing. Which, judging from TV, is pretty much the only thing for a sofa to face.

You expect this kind of conformity in apartments, which are, after all, the least individualized form of shelter available. The door to the hallway is almost always on the right, whether you live alone (*Seinfeld*), have recently moved on up (*The Jeffersons*), are starting a family (*Rhoda, Mad About You*), or are in some situation that defies a brief explanation (*Will & Grace*). The exceptions tend to be people who can't afford an appropriately right-doored apartment (*Good Times*) or who live across the hall from an apartment with a door on the right that's onscreen almost as much as theirs is (*Friends*), or are in some situation that defies a brief explanation (*Frasier*).

Unlike houses, though, aliens would have trouble re-creating extraterrestrial apartment buildings based on the terrestrial representations we've shown them. For instance, I could never figure out how the architects of Monica's apartment on *Friends* drew up the floor plan without being masters of origami. Radiating out clockwise from the living room, you had the eat-in kitchen, which led to the apartment's front door; the bathroom, which despite its cavernous dimensions somehow failed to encroach into the back of Monica's kitchen cabinets; the balcony, which in a token nod to bohemianism was accessible only through a window instead of fancy French doors; the two bedrooms, both of which were as big as the kitchen without spilling over into each other; and a live studio audience of several hundred people. Actually, now that I think about it, aliens are probably the only ones who *could* reconstruct such a space, provided they live in an M. C. Escher dimension where the laws of Euclidean geometry do not apply.

COME IN

Oddly, none of these apartments seem to have security doors. The first time I lived in an apartment, I was constantly expecting people to just knock on my door when they dropped by. How they were supposed to get into the building in the first place was something I never thought about. The whole concept of "buzzing in" is simply not portrayed on television in any kind of meaningful way. People just knock on doors there. And that's if you're lucky. More often they just walk right in. Yes, we understand that when watching TV, people don't always want to have to sit through the unthrilling spectacle of the householder hearing the knock or the buzz, walking across the floor, and letting a visitor in. There are only so many witty and entertaining things people can say while going to the door. *The Single Guy* "solved" this perennial problem by having its protagonist, Johnny, answer every knock at his door with a hollered "It's *always* open!" In New York City? *The Single Guy* barely lasted two seasons, and I always assumed that was because Johnny had been murdered in his home.

There's always the possibility of a hushed, rushed discussion of how to deal with unwelcome visitors, or people hurrying to clean up some mess or hide something embarrassing before letting a guest in. *Rhoda* milked all the possible laughs out of having a goofy, invisible doorman at the other end of the intercom, and then kept doing it so that nobody else ever could again. So, alas, the only valid way to manage visitors on TV is to have them walk right in. All the time. Every time.

If you like privacy in your own home, TV shows us that you're out of luck. The lack of the most basic boundaries in living space has become a central point on any number of shows. As early as *Empty Nest* in the nineties, next-door neighbor Charley regularly made a point of bursting right in through the Westons' back door, barging into their kitchen, and opening their refrigerator before the entry door had even swung shut behind him. *Everybody Loves Raymond* wouldn't have been a quarter of the show it was if the elder Barones, who lived next door, weren't always showing up uninvited. The less said about Kramer's pyrotechnical entrances into Jerry Seinfeld's apartment, the better (even though it's already way too late on that score). And *Buffy the Vampire Slayer* played with it just like it did with every TV convention, when Giles greeted at least one uninvited guest with a bemused mutter of, "Now, I'm *sure* I locked that door this time."

Just locking your door isn't enough either. There are other ways around it, but they aren't any less silly. One of the hooks of *Dawson's Creek* was that Dawson had a ladder leading up to his bedroom window so that Joey could climb up and visit him without having to bother with onerous obstacles like door knockers and doorbells, let alone hallways and staircases. That ladder was supposed to be symbolic of their friendship, how everything between them was open and they could tell each other anything.

But they never explained how Dawson's parents let him get away with it. Go ahead and try the ladder thing if you're a teenager, and see if your parents put up with it.

Joey risked a broken neck every time she stopped by. If she'd had a similar ladder for Dawson to climb up into *her* bedroom, everyone would have been scandalized. And how was their friendship not suspended every spring and fall, when it came time to clean the leaves out of the rain gutters? Anyway, it all ended with a ladder lying in his yard, just waiting to trip someone who would then sue the Leerys for everything they owned. Not worth it on any level.

Perhaps the best solution to handling visitors ever shown onscreen is one where you both live and work in the same building, surrounded by people who exist to serve your every need, a nearly impenetrable envelope of security, and a secretary with an intercom to tell you that your next visitor is waiting right outside the door. But not everyone can live like President Bartlet on *The West Wing*. And even he didn't get to stay there all the way to the end of the series.

ALONE TIME

Real-estate listings always tell you the number of bathrooms on the property. But as we know from TV, it's not the *number* of bathrooms that matters, but the size of the one that you have. That's because nobody's ever in there alone anyway, and the most important thing in a bathroom is the ability to fit at least half of the cast in there at one time. Look at the Bradys, who were able to make a one-bathroom house work for them because they could all congregate in there for family scenes. Which, after all, is what bathrooms are for—having arguments in, hiding from people in, and, very occasionally, waiting impatiently outside in the hallway for. If you want to take a crap, you go someplace private instead.

Which brings us to an important point. I was pretty young— we're talking single digits here—when I first noticed something unusual about the people on television: they never seemed to go to the bathroom in the biological sense.

I was still too unsophisticated to recognize television as anything other than a window into another literal reality, and it was going to be a while yet before I realized that Gary Coleman wasn't coming up with those clever retorts on *Diff'rent Strokes* all by himself, on the spur of the moment. So I recall being curious as to why, even on a gritty, realistic show like *Little House on the Prairie*, nobody ever seemed to hear nature's call.[2]

I never watched *All in the Family* as a kid, so I wasn't aware at the time of the running gag about the toilet flushing offscreen. And I wasn't aware of something else, which is this:

The reason you never see TV characters using the bathroom isn't just that it's "indecent." It's that it's something people do alone. People doing things by themselves alone on TV is boring. You almost never see people doing anything alone, even if it's something people often do by themselves in real life. Cooking, studying, knitting, reading, watching TV, thinking, investigating a homicide, standing at a urinal—they're all things we like to do

---

2. Of course I now recall a scene or two from *Little House*'s syndicated run when I was a little older, in which the exterior of the outhouse made an appearance. Not being old enough to know that Gary Coleman wasn't a natural wit, how was I going to know what an outhouse was?

on our own, but it seems like TV characters can never manage any of them without a partner or three.

And this doesn't only apply to people engaged in cooperative pursuits either. On the contrary, even a lone cop fighting impossible odds in a pitched gun battle shares the scene with the people who are shooting at him. People on TV have no "me time."

That's because TV is nothing without people interacting. You don't get much of that when people are in the bathroom, unless they're standing at adjoining urinals, and frankly I'd rather not encourage people to talk to me when I'm in that position anyway. You might catch an occasional one-man show on PBS or something, but, as stated in the introduction, this isn't a book about what you can learn from watching PBS. You can watch PBS for that.

Now, there are a few rare cases when someone is going about some task all by their lonesome. But even then, they often have to have a voice-over explaining what it is they're doing and why. This is especially common in private-detective circles, from *Magnum P.I.* to *Veronica Mars*, but it's also not unheard of among folks with a TV-unfriendly introspective bent like Carrie Bradshaw on *Sex and the City* or Kevin Arnold from *The Wonder Years*. But there are limitations here as well. Narrative voice-over is a frowned-upon device in writerly circles as it is, so even the most self-regarding character isn't going to push his or her luck by telling a viewing audience, "After sitting there on the throne for longer than I care to admit, I made a mental note to buy bran."

One notable exception was *Ally McBeal*, a show where several scenes a week took place in the unisex bathroom of the Cage Fish law firm. This innovative setting made it possible for characters to interact in the loo without regard to gender. Of course making your employees share a workplace bathroom with people of the opposite sex is also a good way to invite a lawsuit—unless that workplace is a law firm, in which case nobody is inherently more likely to sue anybody else. And it helps if the senior partners are insane, which John Cage and Richard Fish inarguably were. But even in a place that you might think would open up a whole new world of dramatic/scatological possibilities, most of the interactions between characters in the unisex will take place at the sink instead of between urinals or over stall dividers. It's also a perfect place to overhear stuff by hiding in stalls with your feet drawn up on the seat to avoid detection. Just be careful, or you could end up like Ally, that time she fell in and got stuck as a result of being so damn skinny. But the less said about this latter situation, the better, so let's move on.

INNER SPACE

One of the most important things about TV is that interior spaces look bigger than they actually are. Maybe this is the real estate equivalent of "the camera adds ten pounds"; it also adds a hundred square feet. One of the most extreme examples of this phenomenon was *The Love Boat*. Every single stateroom on board the *Pacific Princess*—no matter how rich or poor or stowing-away the passenger or passengers occupying it might have been—seems about as big as a medium-size hotel room. Maybe things were different in the seventies. On my one and only Caribbean cruise, my stateroom was perfectly nice, but attempting to shoot a scene from a TV show in there would have been impossible. There might have been space for the characters *or* the camera, but not both. This was certainly not the case on *The Love Boat.* More's the pity, because most scenes on that show would have been greatly improved if they had consisted only of an extended, extreme close-up shot of the opposite wall.

But it's also noticeable on land, where incredibly spacious homes are occupied by people who really shouldn't be able to afford them. The enormous Manhattan apartment complete with balcony on *Friends,* for instance? Yes, Monica had roommates for most of the run—just about everyone else in the cast, in fact, at one time or another—but the only way she could have actually afforded that place would be if all of them had lived there at the same time. And that's not even taking into account her period of unemployment. Now, we did eventually learn that the apartment was her grandmother's and had been in her family forever, which made it, in Chandler's words, "a friggin' steal." All the more reason that they never, ever should have given it up. Holding on to that place would have been worth a daily commute to and from Ohio.

Or would it? TV has also shown us that even if you're "poor," your home will be enormous, even if it's in a run-down apartment building like the Evanses' on *Good Times.* They were always going on about how destitute they were, living in "the projects" and "the ghetto," but their living room was as big as anyone else's on TV. Granted, they had a shortage of bedrooms that forced J.J. and Michael to sleep in the living room, but at least that living room was big enough that neither of them, not even the freakishly tall J.J., had to sleep with their feet out the window. Maybe the secret is to have a close-knit family and a tight group of friends. That might explain why when everybody was in the same room together, there was always plenty of space for everyone who lived there, plus Wilona and even Bookman, not to mention at least two cameras. And if they never seem to bump into one another, you can probably manage it too.

And look at *7th Heaven*. Nondenominational preacher Eric Camden had to live on the change in the collection plate, so money was always tight. Yet he and his ever-fluctuating brood always seemed to have enough rooms in that giant mansion they lived in. Even when "grown" daughter Lucy moved back in with her husband and infant daughter, there was still space for two entire families in there, and not one of them had to live in the basement. No matter how much any of them deserved to. Whatever your income might be, don't give up on scouting for homes until you've found the right place with plenty of room to host dance parties and Bible-study groups.

Something else to keep in mind, if you ever find yourself shopping for a house, is that you can't judge interior space by looking at the exterior. For instance, on *Too Close for Comfort*, poor Ted Knight as Henry Rush had to live in that ridiculously narrow San Francisco town house. From the outside, it didn't even look wide enough to accommodate his drafting table, let alone his bottomless collection of college sweatshirts. Yet he was able to find space do his work even in the constant presence of his wife, two grown daughters, and whatever the hell Monroe was supposed to be back before gay characters could be on any comedy that wasn't *Soap*. As much as Ted bitched about the constant distractions, it was a miracle that people didn't have to literally crawl over him all the time, like on that *Saturday Night Live* sketch where Chevy Chase and his family lived in a trailer that was parked vertically.

It even applies to the domiciles of people who spend most of their time not in a fixed structure, but in a moving vehicle. Look at B. J. McCay on *B.J. and the Bear.* That show's theme song included the line "best of all I don't pay property tax," which indicated that B.J. was, to all intents and purposes, homeless. Now, for the long-haul trucker, you might expect that even the most spacious cab is going to start feeling pretty claustrophobic after a while. And you might also think that would have to be even more the case if for some reason you have decided, like B.J., to let a chimpanzee ride shotgun. I've never been a professional truck driver, but I've been on my share of road trips, in vehicles ranging in size from a luxury van to a Geo Metro. Alas, none of these journeys has ever included the added pleasure of a screeching, nonverbal sociopath reaching into his pants and flinging poo at me all the time.

But it's clear that if two primates can only find a way to be so cozy in that bench seat for long periods of time, it'll somehow more than pay off in cargo space. I don't know how this works, but the evidence is incontrovertible. Just look at what B.J. carried around in his semi trailer. On various occasions, B.J. pulled different types of equipment out of there, from a hang glider to a motorcycle (complete with helmet). And yet he still somehow managed to get enough loads hauled from one place to another to be able to afford spending long periods of time relaxing and/ or brawling in America's one truck stop.

Public places are just the opposite, however. They may look big on TV, but once you get inside you may find yourself with barely enough room to change your mind. Having been inside both the Manhattan diner that was the basis for Monk's on *Seinfeld* and the Boston pub that was the inspiration for Cheers on

Cheers, I don't know how the larger cast members ever fit into those places, let alone three camera crews and a sound guy.

But nobody lives in those places, at least not indefinitely (the time Norm was holed up in Sam's office while claiming to be traveling the world notwithstanding). People do, however, live in spaceships. But pay no attention to that domestic footage on the NASA channel, which always shows the same angle of the same people floating, big-haired, in some tiny horizontal closet. For some reason, the space agency would have us believe that craft like the Space Shuttle and a Saturn V rocket have an extremely low proportion of living space as a percentage of total mass—something to do with fuel to get the astronauts aloft and then the air and supplies for keeping them alive once they get there. However, you and I know this to be false. On every other TV channel, space travelers from *Star Trek* to *Firefly* get to walk around almost their whole ships without regard for how much of the interior should really be taken up by space-wasters like engines, fuel, and supplies. It's impossible to create any kind of decent feng shui with all that crap in the way anyhow.

Probably the most elegant approach to this issue was on *Doctor Who*, in which the Doctor's time machine was the size of a phone booth on the outside but the size of a large office park on the inside. Everyone was always amazed the first time they stepped inside, and the Doctor would always explain it away as Time Lord technology, but I think he was just coming from a future where televised indoor space had finally evolved to its logical conclusion.

I'm willing to admit that it's not TV's fault that living and working and other spaces look bigger on the screen than they really are. People who make TV want people to like watching it, and nobody wants to sit through a TV show where people are constantly falling over one another and having to precisely choreograph everyday activities like having breakfast, getting dressed, and engaging in highly farcical exits and wacky misunderstandings.

Or maybe I'm reading too much into it. Not to name any names, but perhaps it has something to do with the fact that people are always surprised at how small TV stars really are in person.

DO IT YOURSELF

Another nice thing about houses on TV is how little maintenance they require. I'm not just talking about the lack of clutter, despite the fact that nobody ever cleans unless they've been babysitting for the first time in their lives and thus the place is trashed and now their boss/parent/parole officer is stopping by for an unexpected visit. I'm talking about the condition of the house itself, beneath all the nonclutter and fresh paint and wallpaper.

Hardly anything ever goes wrong with the foundation, or the electrical wiring, or the heating, or even any major appliance. Sure, a windowpane might get knocked out by a stray ball or Frisbee (which the kids shouldn't have been playing with inside in the first place, and neither should Dad), but pretty much the only thing that ever breaks inside a TV domicile is the plumbing.

People have different do-it-yourself specialties. Some folks are excellent at wallpapering, like Graham on *My So-Called Life*. Some people prefer to focus on bathroom tile or building giant entertainment centers, even though they suck at it, like Joey on *Friends*. Some are masters of patching and painting interior walls, while still others are experts at laying carpet. Everyone can manage something around the house.

This is very foolish of them. All you really need to know how to do is fix plumbing. And yet, woefully, the only plumbing that most TV characters seem to know how to do is a) try unsuccessfully to fall asleep while a faucet drips all night, and b) attempt to fix it without first remembering to execute the all-important step of turning off the water under the sink. Apparently there's nothing funnier than a would-be handyperson getting sprayed with a stream of water that makes it look like the bathroom vanity conceals a guy with a fire hose.

It's not just sinks and faucets either. Buffy's basement pipes burst one fine morning (probably because of the freezing temperatures reached in Sunnydale, California), and the Sopranos found their basement flooded almost knee-deep when their water heater broke. And then, despite their positions at opposing ends of the socioeconomic spectrum, both Summerses and Sopranos had to go to unusual lengths to get their problems fixed. The lesson here is that if you're going to learn to fix things around the house, make sure it's plumbing. Take a class or something if you need to. But feel free to skip the unit on toilets because those only overflow in the movies and never on TV.

CONCLUSION

Obviously we have all spent a lot of our time indoors and will continue to do so, if for no other reason than that's where the vast majority of televisions are to be found. That's why people put so much effort and money into the places where they live. Everyone wants to have as much space as possible, even if the space they're most concerned with is the area between the sofa and the TV. But if you're dead set on having a roomy home, consider simply eliminating your fourth wall. It works for absolutely everyone on TV.

Learning Experiences

1 Remodel your home so that your front door is on the right, the stairway is upstage, and the door to the kitchen is stage left. The upper-level floor plan is up to your discretion, but in the interest of protecting your home's interior from the elements during the project, I would suggest timing it so that the lighting grid is absent for the minimum amount of time.

2 Move to New York City, and rent an apartment with a giant living room, two bedrooms, a spacious full bathroom, a balcony, and, if possible, a fireplace. It may seem a challenge to manage this within your price range, but you may find that the complete lack of a security door makes up for the other amenities in negotiating your monthly rate.

3 Try living for a week with your sofa in the center of the living room, always leaving a gap on one side of the kitchen table when your family sits around it, and having everyone face the same direction when you talk. See who has a psychotic break first.

4 Go to the bathroom. While you're in there, observe whether anything happens that would be worth including in a TV show. If anything does, make an appointment with your doctor immediately.

5 Attempt to fix your own plumbing. Don't bother turning off the water before you commence, but it's probably a good idea to have the number of a plumber ready before getting to work. If the number is written in some form of waterproof medium, so much the better.

9

Straightening the Curves, Flattening the Hills

TV Physics

Sir Isaac Newton is rightfully famous as the father of modern physics. With his discovery of gravity, his laws of thermodynamics, his masterwork *Principia*, and his invention of calculus (which, by the way, thanks a lump for that last one, Ike), he laid the foundation for much of our understanding of the way the universe functions on a fundamental level. I confess that I'm not entirely clear on how he accomplished this, and that's because television doesn't generally go into the life of Newton and the significance of his achievements. In many ways, it's as though Newton never existed in the world of television. And you can totally tell by the physics there.

UP, UP, AND AWAY

One of those laws of thermodynamics is that "Every action has an equal and opposite reaction." Or at least I think that's how it goes; again, I'm a little fuzzy on the specifics. But on TV, the interpretation of that law seems to be along the lines of "Every action has an equal and opposite reaction, only way more vertical."

Nowhere was this more apparent than on *The Dukes of Hazzard*. In the Evel Knievel seventies, it didn't seem at all unusual to tune in every Friday night to see an orange Dodge Charger flying through the air. In hindsight, one realizes that Hazzard County must have been named for the ramp-shaped piles of dirt that dotted the roads every half mile or so. The amazing thing wasn't the extent to which vehicular aviation was commonplace, but the fact that they were doing it on purpose.

At least once an episode, we'd expect to see the *General Lee* soaring gracefully into the southern sky, describing a perfect parabolic arc[1] in slow motion while Bo and Luke emitted a tandem rebel yell out the open windows, until the car made a soft landing a dozen or so car-lengths down the road and proceeded on its unimpaired way. Yet somehow, whenever Roscoe or Enos made an ill-advised attempt to follow, things would go wrong. Probably the same things that would go wrong if you or I were to try it.

First of all, there's the fact that it's hard to build up the required escape velocity on a dirt road. Upon reaching the sum-

---

1. Or something like that; see previous references to the amount of science and math I've learned from TV.

mit of the ramp with insufficient speed—say, thirty or forty miles per hour—the weight of the engine in the front of the car would immediately drag the front wheels earthward, causing the car's undercarriage to scrape along the top edge of the ramp and leaching off what little momentum wasn't lost during the sudden uphill climb. The car would hit the ground nose first, having failed to travel a single car-length. The engine would kill, the radiator would burst, the hood and front bumper would crumple like so much origami, the flasher bar would slide loose, and the siren would trail off in an amusingly off-key fashion.

But let's assume that a driver did succeed in making the jump. Without a "catch ramp" at the far end to neutralize the car's downward angle, the front wheels would still hit the ground first, hard. The front bumper would dig into Miz Tisdale's pasture before the back wheels crashed to the earth. The car's suspension and alignment would be catastrophically fucked, as several tons of Detroit-built steel, cast iron, and nonsafety glass settled heavily to the ground. The two Dukes, having undertaken their airborne voyage before the use of seat belts became so commonplace in the late eighties, would experience painful if not debilitating compression of their vertebrae as their bodies made the abrupt transition from free fall to being slammed forcefully down onto the Charger's bench seat. I don't care *how* hard they're holding on to the roll cage, several dozen repetitions of this trick should've had them entering the Boar's Nest in wheelchairs before they were thirty (where they will also no doubt attempt to jump over the speed bumps in the parking lot until Uncle Jesse makes them stop it). So how were they always able to drive on with undiminished speed after doing something to their car that should have totaled it? It probably has something to do with their being good ol' boys.[2]

So how does that law of thermodynamics apply? Well, let's see. The action is the *General Lee* hitting the ramp, the reaction is the *General Lee* flying off the ramp, and the vertical part speaks for itself. In fact, after a few seasons, the vertical aspect took over. Where once the Duke boys would have needed a twenty-foot-tall pile of dirt, in later seasons that vertical lift could be accomplished by something as nontowering as the upslope of a gully, or a partially washed-out bridge, or a parked car, or a curb. Especially during the period when Bo and Luke were replaced by those lightweights Coy and Vance. By the end, all it took to get the *General Lee* into the air was a rolling camera pointed in its direction.

SHE'S GOING TO BLOW!

Nowhere is the vertical nature of TV physics more apparent than in an explosion. According to TV, if you are in close proximity to any sort of detonation whatsoever, the explosion will simply lift you off your feet and send you flying in the opposite direction. Nobody is ever simply flattened or floored. There will always be air time. This will be the case whether the explosion occurs below you, on the same horizontal plane as you, or even directly above you. I can't think of an example of this last, where theoretically the shock wave from an air burst would bounce off the pavement

---

2. Presumably, this status also provided them protection from being arrested for 89,785 counts of reckless driving, 451,568 counts of fleeing an officer, and 7.8 million counts of speeding. I mean, Jesus, it's not like Roscoe didn't know where they lived.

where you are standing and launch you almost all the way into the fireball, but I'm sure it's only a matter of time.

The reason it's so important to understand the physics of explosions is that there are clearly so many of them. Admittedly, for some of us, large explosions are rare enough in our everyday lives that one July night a year we all get into our cars and brave horrible traffic to go look at some. Usually not even from all that close up. And yet on *24*, Jack Bauer is in close proximity to at least three or four explosions per day. For instance, in season six he foiled a suicide bomber on the L.A. subway, but was still hurled up and back by the belated detonation. Later the same "day," he had barricaded himself inside the office of the Russian consul in Los Angeles (don't ask) and probably would have been flung upward if the entry charges planted by the consul's guards hadn't dropped the heavy door directly on top of him. And at the end of the "day," he leaped from an abandoned offshore oil rig just as several Sidewinder missiles were striking it, sending it up in flames and sending Jack up onto a ladder dangling from a handy helicopter. I am not making any of this up.

You're thinking, "Well, of course. This is Jack Bauer we're talking about. Explosions are his element." Fair enough. Leaving aside that it's kind of a crappy "secret agent" who leaves such a wide trail of charred wreckage everywhere he goes, it's not only spies who are subject to these dangers. Clearly, even people in other lines of work—say, for instance, doctors—aren't safe from explosions. Like when Meredith on *Grey's Anatomy*—which is not only a medical show, mind you, but one with a strongly female-skewing audience, for what that's worth—was just down the hall from an exploding bazooka round, and the force of the blast knocked her straight out of her shoes. This despite the fact that the shock wave should have been at least somewhat dispersed by the armor that Dylan the Bomb Squad Guy was wearing at the time (for all the good it did him), not to mention Dylan himself before he became what that same episode taught us is called "pink mist." You might think that instantly aerosolizing a large, dense object like a fully grown human being would eat up a great deal of force, yet there still seemed to be plenty left over to nearly bounce Meredith off the ceiling. So consider yourself forewarned.

And God help you if your car should ever go off the road. If you're lucky, it won't explode on impact. You may have several seconds before the vehicle spontaneously erupts into flames, precious time that you should use to make your escape. However, there is one way to extend the time before the inevitable conflagration, and that is to have a fellow passenger who is either injured or trapped in the wreckage and needs your help. Having this person along could save your life because there's no way that car's going to go up before you've finished pulling them out.

I suppose there's also the option of leaving the trapped or injured person to his or her fate. But nobody—even if gasoline has spilled from the gas tank onto a downed power line that's giving off sparks in a canyon full of natural gas while a mass of red-hot magma approaches—is going to do that, unless we already know they're either evil or the most craven coward in history. Don't be that guy. Don't even waste your time yelling at that guy to help if he is your second passenger. If you're going to rescue a helpless victim from the scene (and you are), then take your time and do it right. The worst-case scenario is that if you're still too close to the inevitable explosion when it finally transpires, the vertical force will simply lift you both up and throw you clear. If you're down in a ravine, you may even be lucky enough to get lifted all the way back up to the roadside, where you'll be picked up by a passing truck driver.

Oh, and if you want to outrun an explosion that has already commenced? You're kind of out of luck if you're on TV, because that never happens on the small screen. There's no budget for it there, you see. Your best bet is to hope your show gets made into a movie, preferably in the nineties when the "outrunning the explosion" stunt was particularly in vogue.[3]

NIELSEN'S THREE LAWS OF TELEDYNAMICS

There are certain things you learn at such an early age that you don't remember even learning them. It's like they're encoded in your DNA, so that you know they're true before you even know *why* they're true. For instance, what goes up must come down. Bodies at rest tend to stay at rest, while bodies in motion tend to stay in motion. Andy Richter's next show will tank. Stuff like that.

Similarly basic rules apply in the world of television. I call them Nielsen's Three Laws of Teledynamics, and they are as follows:

1. An urgent warning will become moot exactly one word before you finish uttering it, because at that point, the event against which you are warning will have already occurred. Examples:

---

3. See *Independence Day, The Long Kiss Goodnight,* and *Chain Reaction.* Or better yet, don't.

Skipper! Watch out for that . . .
Don't slam the . . .
Look out for that open . . .
That's not a safe place for the . . .
Don't drink that . . .

A corollary to the first law is that even though the warning becomes moot just as you utter the penultimate word or phrase, you are still required by the first law to pronounce the final word or phrase. You are further required to say it in a saddened, weary, dutiful tone. To continue the examples outlined above:

. . . tree.
. . . door.
. . . manhole.
. . . old lady in the wheelchair.
. . . urine sample.

And so on.

2. An imitation of an individual will immediately cause that individual to appear directly behind you. In most cases, you will be engaging in the imitation for the entertainment of an audience. Alas, however frantically they may try to warn you when the subject of your lampooning is inevitably conjured into the room by your performance, you will be so into your eerily dead-on rendition that you will only be stopped by the individual him- or herself. Probably at the point in your imitation when you turn

around and see them standing there looking deeply unimpressed.

This law applies most powerfully to people in positions of authority over you (bosses, fathers-in-law, police officers), but can also be effective with a peer-level coworker. And it works no matter how cliché avoidant a show usually is. It happened on *The Cosby Show*, when Elvin suddenly and spontaneously developed an uncanny Cliff impression that produced its subject almost instantly (and quite silently, as is usually the case). It also worked on a second-season episode of *ER*, when Doug Ross's cane-wielding mockery of the walking-impaired Kerry Weaver caused her to somehow appear unnoticed in the room even though all of the entrances were in someone's line of vision. And Jim's deep-voiced impression of the lugubrious Stanley on NBC's *The Office* brought the aforementioned gentleman through the door directly behind him in midspoof. (The rest of Jim's impersonations during that episode weren't quite so effective, and he should count himself lucky.)

It seems to me that this second law could be harnessed. Looking for your boss and can't find him or her anywhere? Missing a friend or loved one? Hoping to meet some admired celebrity? Simply launch into an impression of them—the more mean-spirited the better—and before you know it, there they are. I even have a theory that Rich Little found success not just because of his talent for mimicry, but also because he developed a dead-on impersonation of his agent.

As powerful as the first two laws may seem, they only control the behavior of human beings. Behold the third law, which allows you to control the very weather:

3. A torrential rainstorm can be triggered by someone saying, loudly and clearly, the following seven words: "At least it can't get any worse."

   Meteorologists will go on and on for as long as the newscast's director will let them about low-pressure systems and dew points, but if you turn off the TV when the news comes on—or even if you don't—you know that rain is caused by somebody somewhere foolishly uttering that all-powerful jinx.

   Of course the proper conditions have to be in place for the jinx to be spoken without violating TV conventions, which is when it is at its most effective. It must be uttered at what is seemingly the last in a series of cascading catastrophes. For example, you're late for class. You become stranded in the middle of nowhere. You've just crashed your parents' car into a tree, and the convertible top won't go up any more. One of your friends is freshly gut-shot. And somebody else is wearing your outfit. Here is where you say, "At least it can't get any worse." No sooner will the words leave your mouth than a roll of thunder will sound, right on cue, and a steady, drenching rain will commence all at once as though somebody has turned on a tap (which, in fact, someone has. They're called production assistants).

   Back in the dust-bowl thirties, so-called rainmak-

ers used to con desperate farmers out of their dwin-
dling funds by claiming they could bring much-needed
precipitation to the farmers' drought-stricken crops.
If only TV had existed back then, along with farcical
sequences of events that left people in miserable situations and exposed to the elements. Rainmakers could
have made a lot more money, and they wouldn't have
had to con anybody.

PROJECTILES

Witnesses who don't watch TV always tell the police and the
reporters the same thing—that the sound of a handgun is not so
much a *bang* as a *pop*. But those of us who were educated by TV
know that gunshots are powerfully amplified, probably by plac-
ing a microphone directly inside the weapon's barrel. And even
though we can't see the bullets, it's apparent that they're powerfully attracted to bad guys—especially nameless henchmen—
and almost supernaturally repelled by good guys.[4] In any given
season of *24*, Jack Bauer survives several pitched battles despite
being outgunned and outnumbered, and hardly ever even takes
one to the bulletproof vest.

And when they don't kill instantly, bullets have very different

---

4. If the bullet does hit someone, apparently the FCC's chokehold extends to the physics
of broadcast media as well. In 99 percent of all cases where someone gets shot in the head,
it's a bad guy who does it. But aren't bad guys supposed to have their weapons loaded with
illegal hollow-point bullets that "pancake" on impact and blow out the whole other side of
the skull on exit? Because I'm pretty sure that's what they told me on *CSI*. And yet do you
ever see a bloody hail of skull fragments on TV? You do not. Either the FCC would object to
such a graphic display or TV bullets are just wimpier.

effects on different kinds of people, i.e., good people and bad people. If you're a good guy, a mortal bullet wound will almost always give you time to utter a few poignant last words, usually to your partner or other close compatriot, before your eyes close. And then a single neat line of blood will trickle out of the corner of your mouth, because the last activity to go as your organs shut down is the ability to swallow.

If you're a bad guy, on the other hand, you will hit the ground hard so that everyone *thinks* you're dead, but after a minute or two you'll come to your senses, and when you discover yourself wounded, vulnerable, and on the threshold of death, your last act will never be to repent or ask for help or even to try to draw a few last breaths, but to pick up your dropped gun and squeeze off one or two more surprise shots from the floor, just so everyone will shoot you a few more times to make sure you're good and dead.

The exception to this rule is if you are the kind of bad guy who gets a final speech, in which case we will then learn that you are not so much bad as "in a bad situation," "desperate," and, after your last breath is drawn, frequently "redeemed." All from a little piece of lead entering your body at ballistic velocity. Whichever organ of the human body it is that generates clichés, it must be a very large target. I'm guessing it's the liver.

It's not only bullets that fly so straight and true either. Here's an experiment. Take a kitchen knife outside, where nobody is around, and throw it at a tree. When I attempted this, all that happened was that the handle clunked against the tree trunk and I irritated my wife. Clearly I must be doing something wrong because according to TV, the blade should bury itself in the wood, leaving the handle to vibrate madly at roughly the same orientation as a carpenter's level. I suspect that I would get similarly disappointing results if I tried it with my ax, but I haven't been allowed yet. And I am under strict instructions not to "even think about it" in connection with my circular saw, and I have thus far obeyed (like jamming the blade guard open wouldn't throw off the saw's balance in the first place).

Obviously there was at least one situation on TV where it made sense for an edged weapon to always strike its targets blade-first, but we can't all have Xena's disc-shaped "chakram." Besides, the all-over blades of the latter are compensated for by the fact that Xena never threw it directly at her target; she always had to bounce it off a few trees, the corner of the nearest building, and maybe Gabrielle's staff, before it wreaked havoc among her enemies. And no matter how many things it bounced off, emitting a burst of sparks with each impact, it never seemed to lose any velocity, in terms of either distance or rate of rotation. Right up until the point when, its work done, it would bounce right back to where Xena could catch it, a remarkable achievement in and of itself.[5]

MAKING SENSE(S)

Even more amazing than the way objects travel through the air on television is the way sound does. If you've ever been in

---

[5]. I know she was supposed to be a Warrior Princess and all, but you'd think that given all the practice it must have taken to master this unique weapon, Xena would have been at the very least missing a digit or two (representing a particularly sharp spike in her learning curve) by the time we met her. But no, she was still fully equipped to play the lyre right up until the end of the series. Well, okay, maybe not after she was killed, but probably right up until then.

a heavy snowstorm, you understand how sound can seem to travel differently in certain atmospheric conditions. That's nothing compared to how differently it travels on TV.

Take for instance punches to the face. I don't think I've ever actually heard the sound of a bare fist striking a face in real life, but to judge from what happens when Captain Kirk smacks a Klingon (despite the fact that they're both armed with handheld energy weapons at the time), if you do it right, it's almost as loud as a real-life gunshot (then again, see the previous section on what gunshots really sound like).

And a private conversation, TV shows us, doesn't require the level of privacy you may think it does. Amazingly enough, simply relocating to about ten feet away from the person you don't want to be heard by usually works.[6]

Even more odd is that at parties, where everyone else is supposedly talking in a normal tone of voice, there's always only one conversation you can hear, and it's always the one that's being had by people you know. I'm not sure how to explain this phenomenon. In the very center of Times Square, there's a spot over a subway grate where you can stand, and the noise of the people and the traffic and the Jumbotrons all fade away, to be replaced by the sound of musical bells. I have no idea how this miracle of acoustics works, but it does. Apparently a similar concept is harnessed in every single party scene of every single TV

---

6. This despite the fact that TV shooting sets are eerily quiet places without a trace of white noise, where you can hear if the guy holding a cue card so much as sniffles. A stage whisper in such conditions carries to the back row of the live studio audience, yet somehow the person standing ten feet away doesn't pick up on it. In its way, it's a dramatic convention at least as transparent and silly as the "asides" to the audience that Shakespeare used (or at least I think he did, according to all the television episodes set in high school that taught us that Romeo and Juliet are always being played by people who hate each other . . . at first.)

show ever. It probably helps to have your conversations always take place in the very center of the room, with everyone half turned to face the camera (you *do* have a camera in your living room, right?) instead of one another.

As I've said before, television is also a highly visual medium, which is probably why everyone on it can see so damn well. Seriously, almost no one wears glasses on TV except people over fifty (and even then usually only to read) and the most hopeless of nerds. Unless you fit one of those two demographics, we can assume you have twenty-twenty vision. And don't tell me that everyone's wearing contact lenses, because you see people futzing with them on TV even less than you see them going to the bathroom. Occasionally someone will claim to have dropped one on the floor in a crowded place in order to create some kind of diversion, but invariably they will later admit to never having worn contacts in their lives.

Even in the dark,[7] nobody will ever stumble, or fail to recognize someone once they've shown themselves. Buffy Summers could even easily engage vampires in hand-to-hand combat in the dead of night, in unlit graveyards. And if you are out late at night and you accidentally wake the neighbors with some loud noise, the lights inside the windows of every surrounding house will flick on. The people inside must be thinking, "Uh-oh, there's a burglar or vandal or car thief right outside! I'd better turn on my lights right away so as to not only totally wreck my night vision but also make it impossible for me to see anything but

---

7. In TV productions, nighttime scenes are often shot in daytime so the camera has enough light to see what's going on; darkness is then simulated by putting a filter over the camera lens that turns golden sunlight into bluish shadows. I learned this from an episode of *McCloud*.

my own reflection. The last thing I want to see right now is the approach of a potential intruder. The less I'm able to tell the 911 dispatcher thirty seconds from now, the better." The only explanation for this consistently amazing level of nocturnal vision is that on TV, it's always a full moon (which still doesn't explain how Willow on *Buffy* ever managed to go on a date with her werewolf boyfriend, but every theory has a flaw).

There's never a sign too far to read, never a bit of action that goes unnoticed without an ostentatious display designed to let us know that the would-be witness is gazing fixedly in the opposite direction. Even if you don't have eyes in the back of your head, you apparently must have them in your temples, an invisible mutation allowing drivers of cars to maintain eye contact with passengers for extended periods of time without ever going off the road (unless you do, in which case, see a few pages back to find out how long you have before the car explodes).

Shows like *Baywatch* also teach us that we ought to be able to capture every nuance of action underwater, just like those frequently-submerged-yet-never-masked lifeguards. They were always able to spot a limp, motionless drowning victim through a hundred yards of cloudy, roiling seawater. And probably identify what brand of swimsuit they were wearing as well.

Beyond seeing and hearing, however, TV has a spotty record at best with the other senses. Unless there's an odor-related plot point, chances are slim you'll be doing much smelling of anything.[8] But even on those rare occasions when something

---

8. In theory, there's a way to work around this limitation of the medium. In its second season, *My Name Is Earl* did an episode in "Smellovision," which only served to make it more distracting. Sitcoms are the wrong format for Smellovision anyway. It would make a lot more sense if someone could find a way to do that consistently on the Food Network, or in conjunction with *Top Chef.*

smells bad, it's never enough to simply comment on it; you always have to compete with one another to see who can make the most horrible reaction face. On one episode of *Gilmore Girls*, the whole town of Stars Hollow was inundated with a temporary stench when a trainload of pickles derailed just outside of town. Those people are quirky enough in the absence of a bad smell, but give them a foul miasma to deal with and they turn positively cartoonish.

The rules of taste are, of course, similar to those of smell, except that whenever someone says more than three words about any sort of flavor, it will either be because of incredible deliciousness or in the service of demonstrating what a hopeless cook someone is (as with Rachel's attempt at a trifle on *Friends*, which, according to Ross, "taste[d] like feet!") or, again, it's happening on *Gilmore Girls*. Not that it's any wonder nobody talks about food on most shows, because there is also no time for actual eating (see chapter 8 for more on why boring things we do alone aren't part of TV). Unless, of course, you are *really* hungry, in which case your meal is doomed to be stolen, ruined, or interrupted by a hilarious crisis, such as a food fight. That must be why almost everyone on TV is freakishly thin.[9]

Which leaves touch. If the tongue (which in real life is divided into flavor zones) has had its function oversimplified on TV, that's nothing compared to the tactile sense. As far as I can tell from TV, we can really feel only three things anyway: hot, cold, and kissing. And not much of the first two.

With those five senses covered, that leaves us only two other

---

9. Yes, I know this is also the case for the principals on *Gilmore Girls*, but at least Lorelai's best friend and chef, Sookie, doesn't look like she sends all of her dishes out of the kitchen without knowing what they taste like, if you know what I mean.

senses: the fabled sixth sense, for which you can refer to chapter 12; and common sense, for the lack of which you can refer to every other chapter of this book.

CONCLUSION

The world may seem like a dangerous place, but it's not as bad as it seems. While there may be an abundance of fistfights and gun battles, they're generally loud enough to give you time to get away from them, especially if you're willing to take your car airborne and are prepared to escape the vehicle after it crashes and before it explodes. Really, it couldn't be more obvious.

Learning Experiences

1 Jump your car over a large ramp and see what happens. Better yet, jump a rental car over a large ramp and see what happens. Even better still, have someone else drive a rental car over a large ramp. You'll be in a much better position to see what happens that way anyhow.

2 Test each one of Nielsen's Three Laws of Teledynamics. If possible, test all three at once.

3 Go to a crowded, noisy party and conduct all of your conversations in a normal tone of voice. You are likely to have many conversations, because each one will be very short.

10

Surfing on the Internet
and Zapped to Cyberspace

High Technology

Television lets us visit a world in which anything is possible through the wonder of modern science and electronics. From hacking into a Defense Department server to solving a mystery with Sherlock Holmes on the holodeck of the USS *Enterprise*, TV characters are able to do amazing things with the powerful technology at their fingertips. Which is kind of ironic considering that most of us watching them don't know what half the buttons on our TV remotes do.

RAM THIS

Aren't computers amazing? Fifteen years ago, if someone had told you that one day almost everyone would have a device in their house that displays text in ninety-point font, uses imaginary search engines, and beeps every time it does something, you'd have thought they were crazy. And yet here we are.

In most senses, TV has surprisingly little difficulty keeping up with computer technology. If anything, it's computer technology that has trouble keeping up with TV. Back in the eighties, the whiz kids on the series *Whiz Kids* were doing the kind of *Weird Science* shit on their computers that you still can't do today.[1] For any regular computer user, there must be nothing more liberating, technology-wise, than to be on a show written by someone who doesn't understand the first thing about what computers can't do.

An especially crucial thing I've learned from TV is that hackers can do absolutely anything just by scowling at the computer screen and typing really fast. But don't forget to say the secret password: "we're in!" It's the hacker's equivalent of a computer's beep, an audible indicator that something has been accomplished, except it's the hacker emitting it instead of the computer. And if you can get the beep perfectly synchronized with the verbally delivered news that "we're in," well, there's probably nothing you can't do. Even more nothing than usual. Less than nothing, I'd say. The day we figure out how to make our *computers* say

---

1. This is especially amazing given the fact that the lead on that show, Matthew Laborteaux, had recently played a character on *Little House on the Prairie* who burned down a cabin thanks to his imperfect mastery of the technology behind a kerosene lantern.

"we're in," that will surely be the day that the line between machine and God finally vanishes forever.

As for today's keyboard-bound TV characters, it's informative to watch them and see how computers will work in the next few years. Judging by what we see on 24 (which is, after all, set several years in the future simply by virtue of the fact that two to three years tend to go by between seasons so those poor people can catch a damn nap), using a computer will involve a lot of opening sockets, rebooting servers, cross-referencing databases, and data mining. I can barely picture how they're going to do this without Windows on their systems, instead having to work with some operating system that always seems to have a real-time infrared satellite feed as its wallpaper. But how they plan to get by without ever using a mouse is beyond me. I guess they're just going to have to type even faster.

To be fair, depicting computers realistically on television is a bit more difficult these days, now that more people know how to use them in daily life. There's more pressure to get it right. I think that's why people who are instant messaging on TV always use correct spelling and grammar and type in complete sentences. No other explanation makes sense.

CAN YOU HEAR ME NOW?

TV would be a lot different without telephones. But even though they exist on TV, hardly anyone ever seems to use them. When they want to talk to someone they don't live with, they have to get in their car and drive over to that person's house or office every single time.

Why are TV characters so much more reluctant to use the phone than to go to the trouble of meeting face-to-face? Could it be that they're paralyzed by the fear of the other person hanging up and subjecting them to a dial tone that begins the instant the connection is broken? Here in the real world, you have to wait a few seconds before the dial tone kicks in, and people seem much more inclined to use their phones as a result.

In the old days, people could only call from inside their homes or offices or phone booths, and the cords effectively tied people to the nearest wall. And in even older days, the people on *The Andy Griffith Show* couldn't dial at all and instead had to give verbal instructions to their phones, which were all called "Thelma."

These days, of course, cell phones have revolutionized people's lives, none more than the lives of people on TV. The creators of *The X-Files* freely admitted that they wouldn't have been able to tell the kinds of stories they did if they hadn't been able to equip Mulder and Scully with cell phones. It's hard to dispute the point. Remember that episode where Mulder jumped from a bridge onto the roof of a train passing underneath, and then dropped his phone over the side in the process? As stupid as he looked doing that, pulling the same trick with a phone booth would have looked fucking ridiculous.

The X-Files also poked fun at its own reliance on cell phones as a storytelling convention, as in the flashback episode set in 1989 when Mulder—for no other reason than to make this joke—answered a cell phone the size of a toaster oven. As we saw over the series run, he never did recover from the permanent slouch that toting that thing around must have inflicted on him. He even still has it now, as a completely different character on Showtime's *Californication*.

I suspect that without *The X-Files*, cell phones wouldn't be as prevalent in the real world as they are today. People saw that Mulder and Scully couldn't get through the day without them, so why should *they* have to? Of course what *The X-Files* omitted were all the scenes where Mulder and Scully had to move furniture around in their government-budget motel rooms in order to find a place to plug in their phone chargers, or a single scene with a dropped call, or static that didn't involve a paranormal or extraterrestrial cause for the interference. Even when Mulder was in a boxcar, buried underground, in the middle of the desert, probably miles from the nearest cell phone tower, and possibly bathed in otherworldly radiation, Scully could hear him as well as if she were in the next abandoned boxcar over. Clearly all the bodies inside there with Mulder were not those of Mulder's cell phone network, who must have been alive and well on the surface immediately above him like the giant crowds of service technicians in those Verizon commercials.

Or maybe it's not the cell-phone network, but the FOX network that makes such consistently miraculous reception possible. Years later, on an episode of *24*, a young couple out camping in the desert one night decided to call 911, on the perfectly reasonable grounds that several large segments of *Air Force One* had just rained to earth all around them (not even kidding here). Granted, the wife had to spend a whole commercial break on the "real time" series wandering around with her phone held high in the air, looking for a spot of ground a few inches higher than the rest in hopes of better reception. But once she got a bar, that signal locked in permanently and didn't let go. Even when the couple had to dash for cover in an abandoned power station, they and Jack Bauer could hear one another clear as a bell. Perhaps the giant brick building acted as a natural antenna.

Like the producers of *The X-Files*, the people behind *24* have also been known to say that they never could have told the stories they did without using cell phones, and again, that's a tough one to argue with. Imagine how many fewer terrorist plots Jack Bauer would be able to thwart if he had to stop to find a pay phone every time he needed to check in with the Counter Terrorist Unit. Instead, he can have an emotional cell-phone conversation with his girlfriend while he's riding in a helicopter (which is apparently not *that* deafening) while she's speaking quietly from inside the office, and they can hear each other perfectly clearly.

It wasn't always this way, even a few years ago. Rewatching the 2001 pilot, the dated spectacle of Jack Bauer pulling his car over to the side of the road so he can safely conduct a cell-phone call seems almost hilariously quaint. Do you think the *terrorists* pull over to talk on their cell phones? Of course not. Now Jack doesn't either, and the country is safer for it. It's not like he ever encounters any L.A. traffic to distract him from his conversations anyway.

But if being a superspy isn't in the cards for you, your next best bet for cell-phone coverage is to be one of those aforementioned terrorists on *24*. The terrorists also have their cell phones and they're not afraid to use them against us. Phones that, like Jack's, always seem to have a full complement of signal bars and never need recharging, even when they have a blinky little *Star Wars* restraining bolt attached to them to let us know they're presently untraceable and the call is uninterceptable (even by CTU's magical real-time "call flagging" technology that instantly downloads a recording of a relevant conversation in L.A. to Chloe's desktop at almost the exact moment when they're out of other leads). If

CTU could just disable every cell phone in L.A. except their own every time there's a terrorist threat, their lives would be a lot easier and the show would have to be retitled *1* or *2*.

At the very least, they should limit the terrorists' available minutes a lot more severely. You can tell that that's one area where *24*'s otherwise well-funded terrorists are already feeling a bit of a crunch, because just to shave off a few precious seconds from each call, none of them ever says good-bye when they're done.

TECHNOFORENSICS

The previous section failed to touch on one other issue regarding technology in the service of counterterrorism and law enforcement: cost. All that stuff is expensive, and it's clear that the Counter Terrorist Unit splurges on the best. Nothing less for you and me, the taxpayers who fund this largesse. After all, it's for our protection, so of course the federal government has no trouble paying for all of it.

I'm kidding, of course. The real money's at the county level.

That's the only conclusion that can be drawn from *CSI*, *CSI: Miami*, *CSI: New York*, and, one hopes, eventually *CSI: Muncie*. The dedicated folks in Clark, Miami-Dade, and New York (and eventually Delaware) counties clearly have what it takes to solve crimes: lots and lots of cash.

According to these shows, it's not just that these crime solvers have access to crime labs containing more scientific equipment than NASA sent along on decades' worth of Mars expeditions (even counting the ones that crashed). They also have seemingly unlimited time to perform experiments, and unlimited materials with which to perform them. In past episodes, some of the experiments crime scene investigators have conducted for their education and our entertainment include:

1. A simulated bus-tire blowout, to find out exactly how many miles a giant road cruiser can travel after having choloroform secretly injected into its tire valve. (Answer: from Barstow, Arizona, all the way to the crash site.)
2. A test to see how long a wrapped-up pig carcass would take to decompose, in order to establish the time line of a suspected murder, and not, as one might imagine, to determine whether the ham in the fridge is still safe to eat. (Answer: long enough for Gil and Sara to resolve their differences.)
3. The creation of a life-size mannequin out of ballistic gel that they then stuck behind the wheel of a dead motorist's Jeep to see if it was possible for him to have been electrocuted accidentally. (Answer: It *was* accidental, and on behalf of the taxpayers of Clark County, thanks for using all that expensive material to catch no murderers, guys.)

So is it really a surprise that they have the kind of equipment that allows them to investigate crimes on a molecular level? Presumably in future seasons, the crime lab will be outfitted with a supercollider, allowing our intrepid investigators to reenact events that involved killer gluons and muons.

CSI has even been mocked by the USA Network's *Monk*, in which the eponymous protagonist—whose own crime-solving methods tend more toward the "Encyclopedia Brown meets Rain Man" school—found himself on the set of a *CSI*-like show and spent all his time making fun of the ultraviolet scanners and tiny fiber collections and whatnot. "What planet are they supposed to be on?" Monk wondered derisively. Well, Monk, they're on Planet Network, where money is no object. On the bright side, people like you who live in the upper cable networks probably pay lower taxes.

Obviously, crime solvers on TV also have even better TVs than we do. Thanks to "digital enhancement," it's possible for technicians to take grainy, black-and-white images from a security-camera video and "enhance" it to make a previously unrecognizable face as clear as it would be on an HD-DVD, or render a dirty license plate readable from half a mile away through a tinted store window (and possibly the license plate's novelty frame, just for good measure). The same can be done for sound media, allowing our heroes to take a recording of a staticky 911 call and break it down, one element at a time, to gather clues about where the call was made. This is the kind of digital remastering that, if it were actually possible, would have resulted in a much better version of the Who's *Tommy* album by now.

It's simple, really: first you take out the dispatcher's voice. Then you take out the caller's voice. Then you play back the resulting background noise. Then you take out the background noise from the dispatcher's side of the call. Then you take out the thumping and screaming coming from the kidnapping victim in the trunk of the car. Then you take out the audio of the drive-through cashier identifying the name and location of the fast-food restaurant where the perp stopped for a burger. Hopefully, after clearing out all of this superfluous audio and cross-referencing the time of the call, our investigators will be able to narrow down a location by identifying a rare birdcall or something.

I, ROBOT

One of the biggest areas where TV is far ahead of real life is that of artificial intelligence. Even more so in cases where that artificial intelligence is housed in a body that can walk around and sometimes even trick people into thinking it's human. Has that ever happened to you in real life? Well, obviously you wouldn't know, but somehow I still doubt it.

On TV, you can generally tell that someone is a robot because their movements are stiff, their manner is unemotional, and they speak in an oddly formal way, like Data on *Star Trek: The Next Generation* or Vicki on *Small Wonder*. In real life, you can generally tell that someone is a robot because they are made of metal and plastic and look about as human as an Erector set.

There was a series in the seventies called *Holmes and Yoyo*, about two police detectives, in which one (Holmes) was human, and the other (Yoyo) was a goofy kind of robot. Yoyo looked like a man, but behind his shirt and tie was a collection of gears and wires. You know, just like any other seventies-era robot.

On *Battlestar Galactica* a few years later, nobody was ever going to mistake the Cylons for humans, with their metal armor and oscillating red eye and highly processed voices (which are, frankly, the thing I miss most in the current version). Today's

Battlestar Galactica features Cylons that are such convincing models of humans that you can't tell they're machines even if you cut them open (which people frequently do).

So then, a few years ago, Honda put out a TV commercial that showed the amazing spectacle of an actual robot . . . walking. For something like fifty thousand bucks, you could have a machine of your own that was capable of strolling slowly down your driveway, as long as it isn't too steep. Kind of anti-climactic, to say the least. Maybe a better place to advertise this marvel of technology would've been via a medium that hadn't been telling us for years how commonplace and convincing robots can really be. Like a print ad in *Popular Mechanics*, for instance.

Keep in mind, however, that robots aren't the only place where you can find robotics. For instance, $6 million in 1970s money was just about enough to turn a g-force-shredded astronaut named Steve Austin into a cyborg. We don't know the price tag for either Jaime Sommers on the original *Bionic Woman*, or that of Jaime Sommers in the twenty-first-century remake, but we do know that on the latter show, Jaime's not the only woman who has undergone a few factory upgrades that would void any warranty. That's because she keeps tangling with another product of the same *Pimp My Bride* garage, a nutbar named Sarah Corvus, who keeps killing people. So now that you know that bionic implants can a) be completely seamless and invisible to the naked eye, and b) turn someone into an invincible murderer, what are you to do? Simple. Carry around a device that generates an electromagnetic pulse that shuts down all electronic equipment in the vicinity. Set it off whenever you meet someone new. Watch closely to see which parts of her body stop functioning. Yes, it may be inconvenient, but it's the only way to protect yourself.[2]

COMING SOON

In future decades, people viewing today's high-technology-based TV shows will almost certainly chuckle knowingly at its cluelessness, just as we currently chuckle at stuff that used to be on TV (not that it's possible to find a rerun of *Whiz Kids* anywhere on the air in the English-speaking world). People will probably look at them the same way we look at old issues of *Popular Mechanics*, which in the fifties depicted a future world of personal hovercrafts and elevator commutes to day jobs (or homes) in orbit. But no need to worry; fifty years from now, the only people watching today's TV shows will be aliens who live fifty light-years away and have a) no TV networks or studios of their own, b) really good antennas, and c) a lot of time on their pseudopods.

CONCLUSION

We may wish for technology that doesn't exist yet, or that we know is out there but we can't afford, but on TV, neither of those situations is ever a problem.

On the other hand, remote controls on TV seem kind of tricky. Whenever one is used—whether it be for a TV, a car

---

2. I would also suggest backing up the data on your computer frequently, at an off-site location.

alarm, or a killer robot—it has to be jerked violently every time a button is pressed. So that's kind of a trade-off.

Learning Experiences

1 Learn to type up to three hundred words per minute. At this speed, you should be able to program your home PC to predict earthquakes. If not, learn to type up to four hundred wpm. Continue until satisfied with the results.

2 Working from a recording on your answering machine or voice mail, try to determine who is calling, what time they called, and what they wanted. You must do this after erasing the vocal track.

3 Look for places where your cell phone won't work. Try it in walk-in freezers, elevators, airplanes at cruising altitude, mine shafts, MRI scanners, and your living room. If it works in all these places, let me know. Especially your living room. I'm thinking of switching networks.

4 Build a robot in your garage using Tinkertoys, LEGOs, or an Erector set. Make it as convincing a model of yourself as you possibly can. Do not consider this task complete until you can send it to work in your place without anybody suspecting (extra points if you commute by car).

11

To Boldly Go

Outer Space and Science Fiction

Even if much of what occurs on sci-fi television is literally impossible, as some joyless sticks-in-the-mud claim, there's still a great deal we can learn from the genre. That's because, in order to justify its existence, sci-fi generally deals in allegories that relate to our present-day, earthbound situations. As with much of television, the underlying lesson is this: even in the vast, empty, silent, black reaches of outer space, everything is all about us.

AVOIDING SKYROCKETING BUDGETS

Legend has it that Gene Roddenberry originally pitched the idea for *Star Trek* as *"Wagon Train* in space." At only four words in length, it's an ideal pitch. Of course it wouldn't work today because now you'd have to answer the follow-up question, "What's *Wagon Train*?" Unless you're pitching to a *Star Trek* fan who already knows this anecdote and thus can be relied upon to know that *Wagon Train* was probably something like "*Star Trek* with wagons."

Come to think of it, the "in space" part would probably be considered a major stumbling block as well these days. While the first few episodes of *Star Trek* cost less to produce than an hour of C-SPAN does today (and look like it), it was a very high-budget production for its time. And aside from *Doctor Who* in the seventies, science-fiction series haven't gotten any cheaper to produce since then. But that hasn't prevented anyone from trying.

When NASA sends people into space, they spare no expense. Every eventuality is planned for, every fail-safe backed up with another fail-safe. It runs up the tab in a hurry. And it's totally worth it, because of the five Space Shuttles, three of them have yet to explode.

Television, by contrast, is the opposite of NASA. Everything you see on-screen in a space-based show had to be paid for, so you can tell what they saved money on by what you don't see. On *Doctor Who*, it was convincing aliens and sets. On *Farscape*, it was more than three or four nonpuppet actors. On the original *Battlestar Galactica*, it was scripts. On the new *Battlestar Galactica*, it's laser beams and camera tripods. And on *Star Trek*, it was a practical way to get from the ship to the planet and back.[1] In

---

1. Do you know why the *Star Trek* transporter was invented? It wasn't because it looked cool, or because it was the quickest way to get Kirk and Spock on and off the *Enterprise*, or even so we'd today have the immortal catchphrase "Beam me up, Scotty" (a catchphrase that,

other words, most of what we know about life in outer space is based on how much it costs to put on-screen.

Which is why it's a little strange that *Star Trek* claimed to have aspired to certain standards of realism. The main weapon on that show was originally going to be lasers, but then some scientist told them that lasers have other, non-Klingon-frying uses, so they went with something called phasers instead. And then they painted blue stripes on the film to indicate them. *Bang*, realism accomplished. Feel smarter?

PHYSICS, SCHMYSICS

When dealing with space travel, you have to have some way to get from one place to another in a reasonable length of time. Einstein tells us that it's impossible to travel faster than the speed of light. But TV tells us different. After all, who wants to watch a show about astronauts taking seventy-five years to get to the next star system? I'd rather sit through all seven seasons of *Star Trek: Voyager*.

So obviously there's a way around it. The *Enterprise* and its direct descendants have "warp drive," which is a more descriptive term than its inventors may have realized. According to one of Einstein's theories of relativity (either the General one or the Special one—I haven't seen a TV show yet that tells me which is which), traveling at high speeds distorts time. The closer you

---

like "Play it again, Sam" in *Casablanca*, was never actually uttered in those exact words). It's because the original mode of transportation, the shuttlecraft, was going to be too expensive to routinely film. By this logic, NASA should have started beaming astronauts to the International Space Station years ago.

get to the speed of light, the faster your subjective time goes in relation to that on Earth. The original *Enterprise* departed on its "five-year mission" in the twenty-third century, so you would have to assume that after a half decade of breaking the light barrier, they'd be getting home several hundred millennia in Earth's future, at about the time the last *Star Trek* fan dies. Yet somehow they were able to communicate with Starfleet Command back on Earth in real time. They'd get their orders, and off they'd speed to their new destination. Of course the faster they went, the later they'd be, so it was a good thing they had Scotty in the engine room suspending the laws of physics. It just goes to show that so-called universal constants have no power over the military chain of command.

Scotty and his fellow *Trek* engineers weren't the only ones who knew how to go faster than physics should permit. There are any number of ways to travel interstellar distances in the blink of an eye: "stargates" on *Buck Rogers in the 25th Century*, a "starburst" on *Farscape*, any manner of wormhole-related malarkey on *Deep Space Nine*, and of course the *Galactica*'s FTL drive, FTL standing for "faster than light." Rather a prosaic name for a method of basically teleporting who knows how many light-years, but since nobody ever gets to have any fun on that show anyway, why toss them the bone of letting them say something that sounds cool once in a while?[2] The point is, with so many ways of getting from point A to point Zed-Omega, it's amazing there aren't a lot more deep-space collisions from all the traffic that's warping and jumping and starbursting around.

─────────

2. Okay, that's not actually true. They do get to say fun things like "bingo fuel" and "so say we all" and enough repetitions of the supposedly obscene four-letter word *frak* that one day it will be considered actually obscene.

And none of this would be possible without "inertial dampeners," those handy devices that make it possible to instantly accelerate to supralight speeds without the ship's passengers experiencing a million g's of gravity, enough to squash them into space-suited strawberry jam. Somehow, gravity aboard spaceships always seems to be steady at one g.[3] Whether the ship is zipping away, slowing down, or just hanging in space, the people inside are consistently feeling approximately the same level of gravity that one experiences on a Burbank soundstage.[4] We've never seen what happens when a ship tries to go supralight with the inertial dampeners down, but I suspect it's a lesson we wouldn't soon forget.

Of the few shows that have even bothered to address the gravity situation on board spaceships, most of them have made a passing reference to "artificial gravity" and had done with it. Occasionally you'll hear something about "gravitic plating" in the decks. This is presumably a special kind of flooring that somehow simulates the effects of gravity by pulling objects toward it. We are already on the right track for developing this technology, as a primitive form exists today: carpet that sucks.

---

3. A few films have featured realistic depictions of zero-gravity in space. *2001: A Space Odyssey*, for instance, put its characters on board spaceships where the only gravity came from centrifugal rotation. And for *Apollo 13*, director Ron Howard built a set on an airplane whose flight path can simulate zero gravity for thirty-five seconds at a time. But if you want to see realistic space-gravity—or lack therof—on TV, you're going to have to turn to the NASA channel, which unfortunately is even more boring than *2001: A Space Odyssey*.

4. Except in cases where the ship is struck by something heavy or powerful, in which case the camera tips thirty degrees to the side and the entire cast lurches in that direction.

STAR WARS

As much as *Star Trek* and its spin-offs made a point of using phasers, you'll be behind the times if you try this on any other sci-fi show, every one of which has used lasers. We're all familiar with the brilliantly colored spears of light that hurtle through air or space, sometimes slowly enough for a target to dodge. That's why it was such a disappointment when I got my first laser pointer. Not only did the beam travel at the speed of light (that is to say, fast enough to beat me to the far wall every time), but I couldn't even see it from the side unless I shined it through a cloud of flour or something to diffuse it. Oh well, at least the cats enjoyed chasing it. Except for when they slipped in all the flour on the linoleum.

But at least my laser pointer was never thwarted by a deflector shield. I never knew those things even existed until I was old enough to start listening to dialogue, and even then I had to take the characters' word for it. But then, at some point, deflector shields suddenly and without explanation became visible. Not usually, but whenever they absorbed a hit, an egg-shaped cocoon around the ship being fired upon would light up like St. Elmo's fire. I just wish I knew if this was because of an evolutionary leap in deflector-shield technology in the twenty-fourth century, or a nifty CGI trick that came into common use in the 1990s.

But you've probably heard enough about all this. Even though in space, you're not supposed to be able to hear anything. There's an old urban myth according to which sound doesn't travel in a vacuum, no matter how noisy the laser cannon or how massive the explosion. Which is ridiculous, since all those space-battle scenes have a lot of neato sound effects. I can think of only one show that kept its exterior space scenes completely silent. But *Firefly* not only lasted a mere eleven episodes, it also totally caved when the film version came out. Maybe the film industry has union requirements for using a sound crew that TV doesn't.

I suspect that the reason we can hear sound in space is that it's not actually space, but some kind of atmosphere. That would certainly explain the prevalence of winged craft in stellar skirmishes, even though wings would be useless in a vacuum. Maybe the wings are there to maneuver and help pilots execute those smooth curves and banks we're always seeing? Steering like that in space isn't actually possible with current technology, so maybe they just know something we don't. Which, after all, is why you're reading this book.

ALIEN SOCIOLOGY

One of the most amazing things about the future is the elimination of racism. I'm not just talking about how, over the course of five different *Star Trek* series, black people went from being the communications officer with one or two lines per episode (original series), to the chief engineer (*The Next Generation*), to the captain (*Deep Space Nine*), to the Vulcan sidekick (*Voyager*), to the helmsman with one or two lines per episode (*Enterprise*). I'm not even talking about how each crew included a former "enemy" (a Russian on *TOS*, a Klingon on *TNG*, a Ferengi on *DS9*, a Borg on *Voyager*, and like anybody cares about *Enterprise* anyway).

I'm talking about how racism isn't racism anymore. It's just considered fact. Everybody knows that all Klingons are warlike and honor-driven, all Cardassians are power-hungry fascists, all Ferengi are greedy, all Romulans are really unflatteringly coiffed, on and on ad nauseam. It's not racism if it's the way things really are, right? Besides, time is at a premium on TV, and it saves a lot of character development if you can just tell everything you need to know about a person right away by looking at their facial prosthetics.

But then it's easy for us to make these kinds of assumptions, as the dominant species in the galaxy. Most sci-fi universes have the earth as some kind of political center, and humans the boss of everyone (aside from the occasional fractious race of monsters that needs putting in its place). Of all the planets in all the solar systems in all the galaxies, the one you're on will one day be home to the capital of the United Federation of Planets on *Star Trek*, the capital of the galaxy on *Buck Rogers*, and, according to *Doctor Who*, several of our very own empires over the next few millennia. While this last may be little more than British postimperial wish fulfillment, it makes sense on a basic level. Since we are a race that tends to create God in its own image, it only makes sense that we'd do the same with the whole universe. Both *Battlestar Galactica*s take it a step further, with the crews constantly busting their asses to find the one safe place in the universe: here. Boy, are they in for a letdown.

But in the unlikely event that you ever find yourself in a future that doesn't revere Earth, just do like *Farscape*'s John Crichton, who, upon suddenly finding himself the only human on the far side of the galaxy, immediately started setting about teaching his uneasy crewmates to be more like him. Or, you could end up like Arthur Dent from *The Hitchhiker's Guide to the Galaxy*, a galaxy in which Earth is (well, was, since it got blown up and everything) an unfashionable backwater, and humans are viewed as barely evolved apes. Which, of course, is part of the joke, because come on: like *that* would ever happen. How else do you explain the fact that from Venus to the Magellan cluster, everybody speaks English? You can credit *Star Trek's* universal translators, or *Farscape's* translator microbes, or even Arthur Dent's Babel Fish, but we all know that English will spread its way across the cosmos the same way it did across the planet: by English speakers showing up and kicking some ass.

NOW AND THEN

H. G. Wells published *The Time Machine* in 1895, and despite the fact that his unnamed protagonist was pretty much a detached observer of human history until along about the 8,975th century, time-travel stories have held a certain fascination ever since. Time travel speaks directly to some of the most central questions of the human condition: fate versus free will. Time travel lets us imagine a kind of experimental universe where we can mess with stuff and see what changes, or what can't be changed. It has incredible educational potential. Or at least it would if writers could agree on a consistent set of theories.

Especially *Star Trek* writers. The episode "The City on the Edge of Forever" is widely recognized as one of the best time-travel stories ever broadcast, and almost certainly the best original *Star Trek* episode. It finds Captain Kirk in the 1940s and in love with Joan Collins, playing a twentieth-century woman who Kirk knows must die to ensure an Allied victory in World War II. Kirk grapples with the dilemma throughout the episode, even considers saving her and letting the Allies go fuck themselves. But at the end he does the right thing and lets her get flattened in traffic. History remains intact, and more than a decade later Joan Collins shows up as Alexis Carrington to give *Dynasty* one hell of a shot in the arm.

But *Star Trek* wasn't done with time travel by any means after that episode. There was the one where Spock found himself stranded in the past of another planet, and thus regressed to the cave-Vulcan behavior that his ancestors were indulging in at the time he was visiting. There's the *Next Generation* episode where Data gets his head knocked off in the nineteenth century, but fortunately they've already discovered said head as an archaeological find back on the *Enterprise*, so when Data's body is returned home, it is reunited with its now-centuries-older cranium, on which the warranty has almost certainly expired. *Deep Space Nine* seemed to time-travel every other week, visiting twentieth-century Earth, the original *Enterprise* under Captain Kirk, and, on one mind-bending occasion, a planet populated by their own descendants, who explained that our heroes had been stranded there in the distant past and set up a little colony; then the descendants saved our heroes from that very eventuality, meaning that Captain Sisko and crew were saved by people who, in saving them, ceased to have ever existed themselves. Ouch. *Voyager* encountered temporal anomaly after boring temporal anomaly, and *Enterprise* took us all the way back to a time before the original series even began. Stop me if you're getting a headache here. The one rule about time travel—the lesson we can take away from all this—is that there are no rules. That, and that it must be a lot easier than it looks.

Maybe the most frustrating thing about time travel in the

Trek universe isn't that its rendering was so inconsistent, but that the shows didn't claim to have any answers to the existential questions that time travel raises. You certainly couldn't say the same about a certain other show that had time travel in *every* episode, by which I mean NBC's *Quantum Leap*. This show's protagonist, Dr. Sam Beckett, had invented not only a means of time travel that allowed him to literally inhabit the bodies of others, but also a real-time, holographic videoconferencing system and a supercomputer that could calculate the timestream-repairing purpose of Beckett's every leap.[5] A purpose, by the way, that the show all but stated was set forth by the Almighty Himself. In 1999, no less. Back then I couldn't even get my computer to play Myst II, let alone know the mind of God. Imagine what we could learn from a genius like Beckett, if only he'd return to the present to share his findings. Alas, at the very end of the series, we learned that Beckett never did get to make the long-hoped-for leap home, and presumably lived out the rest of his existence as a transtemporal do-gooder. That'll learn him to try to play God. Karma's one thing, but apparently eating from the tree of knowledge trumps good deeds.

Maybe all we really need to know is that time travel is too important to be left to mere mortals. That's the premise behind the longest-running sci-fi series in television history, the BBC's *Doctor Who*.[6] The not-so-eponymous Doctor was (and is) a member of an alien race known as the Time Lords, and pretty much just lets humans tag along so he can explain things to them. One of these things that doesn't need explaining as much as you might think

5. And all after earning a medical degree, learning how to play the guitar, and writing *Waiting for Godot*.

6. No matter what *Stargate SG-1* might try to tell you at any point in the next fifteen years.

is why the Doctor is always rushing around trying to prevent di-saster when he, you know, has a time machine. That answer has tended to change over the years—it's against the rules, or he can't change things once he's "part of events," whatever that means, or something about the Blinovitch Limitation Effect, whatever *that* is. Naturally, this time traveler has found himself at various critical points in human history, from the end of the planet all the way back to caveman times (with three separate destructions of Atlantis along the way), and he's saved the world in all of them. It's best not to think of the likelihood of his failure on any of these occasions; we already know that the world wasn't de-voured by the Mandragora Helix during the Italian Renaissance, for example. However, on one occasion, the show did make the mistake of addressing this issue head-on, when the Doctor was trying to prevent the assassination of King John before the sign-ing of the Magna Carta. His companion asked what would hap-pen if the Magna Carta weren't signed, and the Doctor assured her that it would be. "But don't you want to see how we pull it off?" he asked. Uh, kind of not anymore, dude.

With its original Saturday-evening time slot, *Doctor Who* was initially conceived as an educational series that would use exciting travels through Earth's history as a teaching device. That's why the first few episodes took young viewers back to caveman times. And then the second story line started teaching us all about the evil pepper-shaker-looking robots called Daleks on the planet Skaro, and from then on kept bringing them back again and again for the next forty-odd years in order to make us smarter and smarter.

In the end, the lesson almost all TV episodes centered around time travel teach us is this: when they're over, we discover that we've somehow been transported thirty minutes to an hour into the future, and we find ourselves in a world where the garbage still needs to be taken out.

THE FUTURE OF THE FUTURE

All sorts of things might be inferred about a culture's mood by looking at how it envisions the future. In the sixties, *Star Trek* was considered "optimistic" simply by virtue of the fact that humanity's continued existence indicated that we might actually survive the twentieth century, contrary to some suggestions. And here we are, although I'm the first to admit that the 1990s eugenics wars (as predicted in the 1967 episode "Space Seed") were pretty rough. In the eighties, Buck Rogers showed us that the future would be one big disco. The nineties gave us (in the person of Sam Beckett) the chance to fix the mistakes of the past. But since 9/11, the future that TV is showing us has become increasingly bleak.

As of this writing, arguably the best sci-fi television series of the moment is the remake of *Battlestar Galactica*. I'm sure that unlike *Star Trek*, this one wasn't sold with a four-word pitch; the only ones I can think of would be "bringing back a stinker" or "post-9/11 in space." A special dispensation for two additional words might allow one to add "total downer."

And that stark view is presented as a very credible one. That's because unlike the original 1970s show, this *Galactica* seems to strive for realism on every possible level, right down to the number of characters who hate one another. There are no deflector shields, and no lasers or phasers to penetrate them if there were;

just good old-fashioned bullets and missiles. Spaceships appear to coast through the vacuum unfettered from the limitations of winged aerodynamics, able to fly sideways or backward. There are no tractor beams, and time travel is limited to the occasional flashback for storytelling purposes. There are no alien races; only Cylons, many of whom are unique individuals despite the fact that there are thousands of identical copies who can infiltrate humanity like terrorist sleeper cells of one. Even the camera work is that shaky documentary style we've come to recognize as "gritty" ever since *NYPD Blue*.

But even *B*G* (as nobody calls it but me) isn't immune to temptation. Explosions in space are still audible, albeit muted as though they're occurring underwater. And cast members walk around comfortably in one g of gravity, even though there isn't a centrifuge to be seen. Maybe we can cut them some slack on this last, however. In the absence of gravity, perhaps they're simply making do with gravitas.

In other words, perhaps there's hope for humanity after all. If we can one day figure out how to walk normally on a ship that doesn't have a centrifuge, perhaps we can stop killing one another. Or, failing that, keep killing one another until there are only forty thousand or so of us left and we have no choice but to start trying to get along. I call first dibs on being one of the forty thousand, by the way.

CONCLUSION

Science fiction on TV is a genre in which many familiar rules simply don't apply. People can travel through space and time, encounter alien races, even conquer death itself. The goal is to push it out there as far as you can, until everything is as new and as unfamiliar and as shocking as it can possibly be. Because then, and only then, is when things get relevant.

Learning Experiences

1 Determine which is more outmoded: the flintlock pistol or the laser beam. Have a duel where one person is given a period weapon that uses loose powder and fires musket balls, and the other person is given a laser pointer. Try not to be the one using the laser pointer.

2 Change the date and time on your computer and send yourself e-mails from the future so you know what to expect. You could also send yourself e-mails from the past, but you'll already know what you wrote.

3 Modify your home computer to know the mind of God. After you've finished, you'll probably want to stop using that one to download Internet porn.

4 Travel to someplace where nobody within a hundred miles speaks a word of English, just to see what it's really like to communicate with a member of an extraterrestrial race. And if you've succeeded in finding such a place, you're probably off the planet anyway.

12

~~~~

Somebody Save Me

Superpowers and Magic Spells

I magine if you could fly. Or if you were impervious to injury, or could do magic spells, or could travel through time, or could solve murders by having visions or by waking up the victims for a minute so you could just ask them. All of us have thought at one time or another how much easier our lives would be if we had special powers, usually when we need them most. The ability to teleport to work when you've overslept. The ability to wiggle your nose and instantly have a clean house when your parents are on their way over. The ability to beat the crap out of rude assholes at movie theaters (or maybe that last one is just me). Everyone imagines how wonderful it would be if we could literally do anything we wanted.

Fortunately, TV is here to show us just exactly how much that would actually suck.

THE EARLY DAYS

It wasn't always this way. On the old 1950s *Superman* TV series, the Man of Steel always seemed to be having a great time schlubbing around in his gray wool tights that fit him like a full-length sweater. And it certainly wasn't because he was meeting his full potential and thus reaching maximum levels of self-actualization. Superman is almost literally a god among men in the comic books, taking on giant mutants, all-powerful aliens, and the binding forces of the universe itself. And yet jolly, jowly George Reeves seemed content to foil bank robbers and income tax evaders. Maybe he was in a better mood then because Clark Kent hadn't yet become the hopeless nerd that Christopher Reeve made him into in the 1970s and 1980s. Maybe it was because the fifties were a simpler time, and thus the most tangled moral dilemma Superman ever had to face was whether to save Lois before or after catching the bad guy. Or maybe it was just because George Reeves never let the expectation of a superhuman physique keep him from making another trip to the craft services table.

SHE-ROES

But as with everything else, what was simple in the fifties became more complicated in the sixties. Thus women started getting superpowers as well, and their men couldn't handle it.

Exhibits A and B of this phenomenon are the contemporaneous paranoid castration fantasies *I Dream of Jeannie* and *Bewitched.* Both Major Tony Nelson in the former and Darrin Stevens in the latter had the terrible misfortune to be saddled with nearly all-powerful helpmates, whom they totally didn't appreciate. Of course the actual women in question were quite different from each other. Jeannie insisted on calling her astronaut boyfriend "Master" (which is the kind of creepy that one doesn't usually encounter outside of certain after-hours clubs) and was supposedly committed to obeying his every wish. This is already a recipe for dysfunction, even before you factor in that Major Nelson's every wish seemed to involve Jeannie not being so awesome all the time. Seriously, dude, the chick can do whatever she wants. If you want to go to the moon, why go to the time, trouble, and inconvenience of all that NASA training when the hot blonde in the harem-girl outfit can literally put you there with a blink of her eyes? Sure, she might forget your space suit, but unless your attitude changes toot-sweet, it would serve you right anyway.

Same deal with Samantha Stevens from *Bewitched.* At least her husband didn't completely isolate her from her family of origin (despite all his endless bitching about them). But aside from that, he seemed to react to having a female mage in the house the same way Major Asshole did: Stop with the magic, woman, I'm trying to impress my boss. If Darrin had put half as much effort into his actual job as he put into keeping Larry Tate in the dark about his wife's powers, he'd have been vice president of that advertising company by the end of the first season. Alternately, he could have relaxed, let his wife take care of him, and ended up as vice president of the advertising company by the simple expedient of having Sam nose-wiggle an air embolism for ol' Larry.

Bewitched is frequently given credit for being more "liberated" (to use a dated term) than its sister show. I'm not so sure. Sam frequently struggled with the pressure of belonging to two different worlds. And as much as she tried to deal with her husband's unreasonable demands, at least she had the cojones to stand up to him once in a while, whereas Jeannie lounged around the house like a fetish model and supposedly devoted her existence to Tony's happiness. Or did she? I've always suspected that her bubbleheaded grin and eager obedience disguised a seething, poisonous rage. Remember, Darrin Stevens, as played by Dick York, eventually escaped his predicament, only to be immediately replaced by a nearly exact replica in the form of Dick Sargent. Tony was denied even that small mercy. Besides, how many other women do you know who will leave a room by literally turning into smoke? That's not the exit of a happy person.

Things got a little better years later when *Wonder Woman* came along, but not a whole lot, and not for very long. The series with Lynda Carter as the titular superhero (and her slightly less titular alter ego, Diana Prince) only lasted three seasons. More importantly, despite its cult status, it wasn't very good. Not least of all because between seasons one and two, Wonder Woman time-leaped about thirty years from World War II to the seventies without looking a day older. Which is a superpower that many people of both genders would envy.

FUN IS FOR MORTALS

In any case, both Darrin and Tony have an awful lot to answer for, since it was pretty much them who showed us, more or less for good, that superpowers aren't all that much fun after all. Once they were finished hiding their women's supernatural lights under a patriarchal bushel, nobody on TV ever really appreciated their own superabilities again.

Even Batman didn't get to have any fun in the sixties. During a time of free love and easy access to drugs, Bruce Wayne had a swinging bachelor pad, a sweet ride, and probably as much offscreen gay sex as his "youthful ward" Dick Grayson could handle. Having a secret identity on top of it all should have been just icing on the cake. And yet he spent all his time getting into fistfights with musical-theater refugees and keeping secrets from his dizzy old aunt. Even when he got the chance to put on the cowl and cut loose, he was still an uptight stick-in-the-mud, always talking like a college professor specializing in public-service announcements. It's well known that Batman wasn't born with any superpowers, and only developed his amazing abilities through hard work, discipline, the investment of millions of dollars, and allowing himself to have no fun whatsoever. Some viewers may be inspired to attempt the same thing, but they should be warned that once you've attained superhero status it is apparently a very difficult habit to get rid of. And what's the point, if you can't even enjoy a beer after a hard day of vigilante-ing?

And Batman was hardly the only DC superhero affected. We never have gotten another TV series with the name "Superman" in the title again, and it wasn't for lack of subject matter. In the nineties, *Lois & Clark—The New Adventures of Superman* (subtitles don't count) was more about the guy in the pinstripe suit than the guy in the red-and-blue one. Who would choose to spend most of his time as a mild-mannered reporter instead of a superhero, as Dean Cain did? Someone who doesn't much like being a superhero, that's who. Which sends a clear message: maybe being a superhero is really all it's cracked up to be.

MODERN SUPERPROBLEMS

If you want no-strings-attached superpowers after the sixties, you're out of luck. Things just kept getting gloomier for the preternaturally powerful, all the way into the nineties. For instance, *Charmed* was about sister witches in San Francisco living glamorous lives in the big city, ensconced in a house that even they called a "manor," and empowered to protect innocents by vanquishing supernatural beasties. But really, all they ever did was whine about it. Oh, boo-hoo, this is such a huge responsibility. Alas, what if someone finds out the truth about us? Oh dear, my husband has turned evil again, and after he tries to sell me to the devil he's going to go play a plastic surgeon on some crap F/X show (Phoebe). Poor me, I'm dead (Prue). Good God, look at my hair (Paige). Who am I again? (Piper). And on and on. The only things these three and a half sisters hated worse than being all-powerful were the occasions when they were somehow temporarily deprived of their powers. Good thing this only happened every other week or so.

The one TV superhero I can think of who really did get a raw deal was Buffy Summers on, what else, *Buffy the Vampire Slayer*.

Her powers were so unspectacular, they didn't even come with special effects and she had to make do with a mere stunt double. On the upside, she was endowed with the strength, speed, and stamina to fight vampires hand to hand. On the downside, she had to fight vampires hand to hand.

Her ancillary abilities were mixed blessings at best. She would occasionally have prophetic dreams that were fairly terrifying yet didn't actually give her enough information to prevent any oncoming horrors. And she had the ability to heal quickly, but for that one to really work, she had to be wounded first. Fast healing is well and good, but if she'd had her druthers, I suspect she would have preferred the ability to not get wounded in the first place. And from the beginning, we knew *that* was off the table; the show kept telling us that Slayers have notoriously short life expectancies. Indeed, in her six-and-a-half year run, even Buffy never could seem to keep from dying for more than a few years at a time. And she had her own show.

Still, that doesn't come close to her ex-boyfriend, the protagonist of his own spin-off, who died centuries before his pilot even aired. Angel (of the series *Angel*) started out in L.A. as a vampire private detective, which is almost ingeniously simple. But when you work in the limitations on vampires that Buffy had been building over the previous four seasons, things got a little more complicated, especially considering the line of work Angel chose for himself. For instance, he couldn't work daytime hours. He couldn't enter homes without an invitation, let alone without a warrant. He couldn't beat people up without turning really ugly first. And a stake in the heart, a beheading, or direct sunlight would turn him into dust. Can you imagine the Hawaii-based Thomas Magnum having to work under such conditions?

That guy got up and walked it off after at least seven beheadings that I can think of off the top of my head.[1] Plus Angel had to deal with the fact that he'd had to break up with Buffy, the love of his unlife, for her own good. Not to mention that every case he handled ended up having some kind of supernatural underpinning. Not once did he ever catch a simple insurance scammer or philandering husband. It was as if Shaft had only been allowed to take on "black" cases. And behind it all was the fact that Gypsies had cursed Angel with a soul, after about a century of terror and torture, which made him feel really bad about everything and drove him to constantly search for redemption. Plus nobody ever seemed to pay him. The real mystery behind Angel's constant misery is why he wasn't in an even worse mood all the time.

Beware, however; you may get superpowers and yet not even get to be a hero. Think about it. There seem to be a lot more evil ones to fight than good ones to win. On *The X-Files*, Mulder and Scully had to face off against any number of supernatural creatures without possessing any special powers of their own. In addition to malevolent vampires and voodoo masters, they had to deal with a guy who could stretch himself enough to sneak through walls and plumbing; a human tumor with the ability to spontaneously regenerate himself; an underachiever with the ability to form his face into a perfect imitation of anyone; and a guy who could talk anyone into doing anything, up to and including suicide. And every single one of these people was a total asshole. But ask yourself this: If the universe bestows you with superpowers, and the choice to either be miserable all the time or enjoy yourself at the nightmarish expense of others, which are you going to pick?

---

1. Not really.

On TV, the former are in a serious minority. A few years after the debuts of *Angel* and *Buffy*, and on the same network, we were introduced to any number of people at Smallville High School who had had insane powers thrust upon them as a result of a toxic meteor shower years before. And were they all villains? Yes, every last one of them, except, of course, for the most super-powered one of them all, who, not coincidentally, had been a passenger in the aforementioned meteor shower.

In addition to not being a murderous beastie, *Smallville*'s Clark Kent had superstrength, superspeed, and total invulner-ability as long as he steered clear of glowing green rocks. Everything a teenager could ask for, in other words. In which case, why was he so damn mopey all the time? Seriously, the most athletic kid at any high school is supposed to have it made, not wind up scarecrowed to a fence post like the victim of some kind of hate crime (as he was in the pilot). Surely, however, as Clark grew into his powers and discovered his destiny, he would cheer up, right? Wrong. Seven seasons in, Clark continues to be a tiresome self-pity case. At least *Smallville* has addressed the question of why Superman always pretends to be such a loser when he's being Clark Kent. The answer? He isn't pretending. Despite being strong, good-looking, nearly all-powerful and in-vulnerable, the most amazing superpower of all—that almost all superheroes share—is the superhuman ability to feel really sorry for themselves.

By way of illustration, let's look at one other thing that Buffy Summers and Clark Kent have in common, besides super-powers and shows on a crappy little network: they've both had sixth-season alternate-reality experiences in which they thought that their superpowers—and the entire runs of their respective shows—were nothing more than their own hallucinations, and they were in fact spending all of their time in mental institutions as a result of being crazy enough to think they had superpowers. In both cases, these alternate realities were presented as being darkly tempting to our heroes, as though being denied essential freedoms and forced to take psychotropic drugs while being incarcerated as a danger to oneself and others were preferable to being superhuman.

The German philosopher Friedrich Nietzsche wrote about the existence of the *übermensch*, literally translated as "superman." In Neitzsche's theory, such beings are above traditional morality as a result of their powerful attributes. And he may be right, if traditional morality doesn't include self-pity.

BEST OF THE REST

Hero malaise isn't even confined to the modern era. If you go further back in time—like, way back, all the way back to the time of Hercules, you'll meet . . . well, Hercules. As played by Kevin Sorbo, the hero of *Hercules: The Legendary Journeys* got to enjoy the strength of a half god without having to walk around looking like a juiced-up steroid case all the time (although those pants of his looked like they'd been split so many times there was nothing left of them but stitches and laces). But did he enjoy it? He did not. He was always having to fight with even stronger giant beasties, and with his full-god siblings and relatives. It's a shame that he didn't live in the modern era, where he could have had a much happier life schlepping around beer kegs and telephone poles and shit like that on ESPN2 all the time. Instead, he had to spend all of his time outwitting his stronger enemies. What the hell is the point of being Hercules if you still have to use your brain? Screw that. In fact, that's why I don't bother working out.

Similarly, the star of his spin-off/sister show *seemed* to be having a good time somersaulting and ululating and mowing down extras like tenpins. And, okay, technically she wasn't a superhero, but come on. You don't leap onto a passing ship from land, like Xena once did, without having some kind of mojo. But every time *Xena: Warrior Princess* had time to take a break, all we ever got to hear about was how bad she felt about all the things she used to do when she was evil. In fact, one of her victims, Callisto (not to be mistaken for the nymph of Greek mythology or the moon of Saturn), had an epic beef with Xena over the death of her own family by the previously evil warrior princess, and it nearly got Xena killed several times. So, like Batman, Xena serves as a cautionary tale about what you should or should not be willing to do in the course of becoming superpowered. But in this case, the message is that you should avoid looting and pillaging and thieving and killing people whose children will grow up to be really pissed off at you.

Another supposed nonsuperhero was Sydney Bristow on *Alias*. Like Xena and Batman, Sydney didn't have anything we typically recognize as superpowers beyond the ability to kick a metric ton of ass. But let's look at this more closely. In addition to knowing dozens of languages and almost as many forms of martial arts, Sydney had the ability to travel halfway around the world on a moment's notice, carry out a mission, and come back—all while maintaining the secret identity of a "graduate student." Anybody who has ever been around a graduate student in real life knows that the time-consuming demands of their academic life make it almost impossible for them to feed themselves, let alone chase Renaissance scrolls all over the planet during breaks from their dissertations. So clearly Syd had a little something going on in the superpower department. Yet she was always too busy working on her trust issues, her daddy issues, and her the-love-of-my-life-married-someone-else-while-I-was-in-a-coma issues to ever really get off on her own awesomeness. And the most important thing Syd ever taught us was in the very first season: no matter how much you trust your civilian boyfriend, or no matter how much he trusts you, don't tell him about your secret life. It'll only freak him out. Okay, freak him out and then get him killed. Which is really not any better for either of you.

HIGHER POWERS

But maybe the problem with all these mopey superheroes is that their powers were just too physical. Perhaps the joy starts to drain out of it once you've slain your hundredth vampire or vanquished your hundredth demon or made your hundredth living-room mess disappear with whatever your trademark facial tic happens to be. Certainly there must be some higher power (so to speak) that would continue to bring joy indefinitely to he or she who wields it, right?

Well, no. In 2003, we met a teenager named Joan Girardi who lived in the town of Arcadia and could talk to God. Not that there's anything unusual about that; lots of people talk to God on a daily basis. However, on the ever-so-cleverly titled *Joan of*

Arcadia, God talked back. He tended to appear to her as a cute guy, a janitor, a dude in a hot-dog suit, whatever was convenient. She always knew it was God by the way total strangers would address her by her first name and frequently make some embarrassing comment regarding something that only she would know. Even so, having a direct line to the Almighty should make up for a few awkward moments, right?

Wrong. Joan got a raw deal coming and going. God was always making her do stuff she never would have done on her own, like joining the diving team or making friends with people she hated or whatnot, which kept making people in her life wonder if she wasn't a little bit crazy. The idea was to teach her valuable lessons on life and make her a better person, but Joan was usually more concerned with typical teen worries—popularity, her irritating boyfriend, her paraplegic older brother (which, okay, was a little bit atypical)—as well as being thunderingly literal-minded, which didn't make her the best vessel for God's teachings. One wonders why He was so patient with her all the time. And unlike Clark and Buffy, Joan's "am I crazy or has all this really been happening?" epiphany came at the end of season one, not halfway through the sixth. Also unlike Clark and Buffy, Joan didn't *get* a sixth season. Just when things were becoming interesting as the show introduced her potential opposite number, patience with Joan finally ran out. Not God's, mind you, but CBS's. *Joan of Arcadia* only got two seasons before being canceled at the stake. The story serves as proof that having God on your side doesn't necessarily translate to popularity among humans just like it says in the Good Book. And on rare occasions like this when the teachings of TV agree with those of the Bible, you know they can't both be wrong.

Oddly enough, the show that took over Joan's time slot wasn't entirely dissimilar, other than being really, really bad. The presence of Jennifer Love Hewitt is almost never a sign of a quality show, and *The Boob Whisperer*—excuse me, *The Ghost Whisperer*—is no exception. Unlike Joan, pretty much everyone in Melinda's life knows about her ability to see dead people. It's easier for them, though; they all saw *The Sixth Sense*, whereas very few of Joan Girardi's high school buddies know a whole lot about prophets. Melinda's deal is that she sees ghosts, and helps them resolve whatever issues they have left over from their corporeal lives so that they'll quit bugging her and make room for next week's annoying specter. She handles it all with aplomb, drawing on a compassionate expression, New Age hippie-dippiness, and a pool of supportive and understanding friends, her husband chief among them. She does deserve props for never seeming to freak out in the face of allegedly creepy ectoplasmic displays that push the envelope of eight-o'clock Eastern Time broadcast standards (or, more accurately, those of the Disney Channel).

Melinda's season-ending twist for the first year came when a friend of hers named Andrea was waiting with her to hear if her fiancé had been killed in a plane crash. And then, when the fiancé showed up, safe and sound, Melinda suddenly tuned out Andrea and started talking about Andrea's death to the fiancé, right in front of her. Nice way to break the news there. Maybe Melinda's equanimity in the face of her responsibility to the dead is outweighed by what a completely horrible friend she is. And we get yet another example of how people with superhuman abilities tend to turn into jerk-offs.

A much better example of balancing paranormal visions with domestic life is seen on *Medium,* which is, not coincidentally, a much better show.[2] Allison Dubois is a happily married wife and mother who just happens to assist the Phoenix police in murder investigations. Not with forensics or detective training, but by seeing ghosts and then telling the cops what she's found out. Impossible, you say? Well, since Allison is based on a real person (namely, a Phoenix wife/mother/medium named Allison Dubois), I can only assume that every episode is based on a true story. In fact, we may be getting dangerously into documentary territory here. The big lesson of *Medium*? If you have a stable, happy family life, there's literally nothing you can't do—including solving murders by interviewing the victims.[3]

WE'RE ALL IN THIS TOGETHER

Most of the shows I've been talking about so far have been about only one person with special abilities, or one tight-knit group like the Scooby Gang on *Buffy* or the Halliwell sisters on *Charmed*. But in 2006, NBC introduced a show in which people *without* superpowers are the ones in the minority. I'm talking, of course, about *Heroes*.

Heroes creator Tim Kring claims not to be a comic-book fan, which is the only way he could credibly state that he didn't steal *Heroes'* "future of humanity represented by select few with superhero mutations" theme wholesale from *The X-Men* (not just the movies, but the comic book that's been running since the

---

2. Patricia Arquette's dreamy "vision face" is way better than Jennifer Lowe Hewitt's as well.

3. For another example of this underutilized investigation technique, refer to the discussion of *Pushing Daisies* in chapter 14.

seventies). Along with the mutation motif in *Heroes* comes the sense of alienation that accompanies the ability to do the seemingly impossible, no matter how awesome it is.

And we've learned from *Heroes* that mutations *are* invariably awesome. If you confine your interest in mutations to science magazines, you'll be stuck with boring stuff like three-legged frogs and bacteria who laugh at your Clorox wipes. Outside of TV, a webbed toe is a mutation. A double-jointed elbow is a mutation. Kelly Ripa is a mutation. On *Heroes*, a mutation is a highly specific ability to defy or suspend certain basic laws of physics. How lucky for everyone on that show that they didn't get stuck with more mundane alterations in their DNA that resulted in things like the inability to balance a checkbook or a susceptibility to hemorrhoids. Because come on, who would watch *that* show?

And yet, despite the fact that they're magically awesome, almost all of them are such downers about it. Cheerleader Claire Bennet should be enjoying her status as a member of the in-crowd already (since, as previously mentioned, hello, she's a cheerleader). Discovering that she's literally indestructible should have only made it better. I mean, she's almost certainly the only cheerleader in her conference who can execute a high-altitude basket toss without bothering to have someone in place to catch her. Yet the first thing she does with her power is begin starring in abortive snuff videos shot by her geeky friend. And she's also probably the only person in history who wasn't incredibly relieved to find themselves waking up on an autopsy slab. Not being dead makes up for a great deal of having to run home naked. Yet Claire still seems so mopey all the time, even when she's in full "spirit" garb.

It's true that some of the other "Heroes" have reasons to be brought down by their abilities. Nathan can fly, but he asks a fair question when he wonders, "What am I supposed to do when I get there?" D.L. could "phase" through walls and other objects, which probably made him feel really stupid about how much time he had spent in a prison that he could have just walked out of. Isaac had the ability to paint the future, but to do so he had to be high on heroin, which gets expensive. And Niki didn't even have any powers of her own, just an alternate personality who kept killing people all the time. Lengthy blackouts that end with your fingerprints all over grisly crime scenes are nobody's idea of a good time.

In fact, the only one who ever really seemed to enjoy his powers was Japanese *Star Trek* geek Hiro, who was rightfully jazzed at his ability to squeeze his eyes shut in Tokyo and open them in Times Square. Then it turned out that Hiro could travel not only in space but also time, which is even better. But then he had to ruin it by embarking on a quest to discover the meaning of his power, and also his fancy samurai sword that Peter saw Hiro's future self carrying for some reason. When his girlfriend died and he failed to kill Sylar, even Hiro couldn't be counted on to maintain a decent mood.

CONCLUSION

It all has to mean something. Could it be that super, supernatural, and magical abilities are actually more trouble than they're worth? With great power comes great responsibility—responsibility that makes it tough to have a proper personal life.

You end up spending all your spare time coddling the fragile mortals in your life and their even more fragile egos, in between acting as a magnet for a slew of enemies that are more powerful than you are. Maybe the ability that superheroes really need, and almost always lack, is the ability to be comfortable in their own skin, with their own destiny, and with who they really are. In lacking that ability, they're more like the rest of us than we may have thought.

Or maybe that's just what they want us to think.

Learning Experiences

1 Develop a superpower. It may be complete invulnerability, or it may be the ability to make a perfect crème brûlée. TV superheroes don't always get to be picky, so you probably can't either.

2 Learn to avoid your fatal weaknesses at all costs. This will unfortunately require you to discover said fatal weaknesses, which can be a painful process of trial and error. I will save you considerable time, heartache, and expense by telling you right now that bullets are probably among them.

3 Create a secret identity. Live your daily life as that person—working, living, and moving among an oblivious citizenry. And then tell me how you got a fake Social Security number, references to get a good job, and car insurance.

13

A Different World
Than Where You Come From

Spinning Off to a New Life

Most science-fiction shows have a little science in them, which is how I learned about how reproduction works. I don't mean in the dirty sense; we didn't have those channels when I was growing up. I'm referring to the propagation of species and the life cycle of organisms. The successful ones live long enough and attract enough positive attention to generate offspring. The unsuccessful ones don't. It's as simple as that. Circle of life, etc.

Some organisms, like insects or fish, have literally millions of children. Others, like us humans, frequently only have one or two, and sometimes none. But what do you call something that isn't likely to reproduce at all, and doing so would make it an exception rather than the rule? You call it a TV show.

And what about a show that produces more than one child in its lifetime? We can count those rare beasts on our fingers, and they include monsters like *All in the Family, Happy Days, The Mary Tyler Moore Show, Law & Order,* and *CSI.* And as we may judge parents by their children, we may judge these shows by their spin-offs. And vice versa.

It's getting harder and harder these days to launch grown children into the world, as witnessed by the short-lived slacker-at-home comedies *Get a Life* and *The Winner.* And it seems to be getting harder to launch proper spin-offs as well; at least for a while there, shows didn't seem to do it as often as they used to. But now the practice is experiencing a kind of resurgence, and there are lessons for all of us there.

For those trying to ensure a soft landing for themselves when they finally leave the nest, we can look at how some spin-offs have succeeded. And for those hoping to help their not-so-baby birds spread their wings, we can look at a few examples of parent shows gently releasing their fragile spin-offs into the world and then yanking all support right out from under them. Everybody wins.

But don't get your hopes up too high. Most spin-offs don't last all that long. And you'd be amazed at how few of them get to move back home.

EATING THEIR YOUNG

It's not considered polite to refer to a television spin-off as another show's "child." That's probably because it's seen as poor form to kill them, which is what happens to most spin-offs. And soon.

Indeed, the life expectancy of a modern spin-off isn't much better than that of a human child was in *Little House on the Prairie* days, when childbirth was a crapshoot and high infant-mortality statistics ensured that said prairie wasn't going to turn into the Twin Cities metro area for a good long time. Only the strongest and hardiest survived, and it's the same way for spin-offs today. If you couldn't go right to work in the rainy, muddy, malaria-ridden fields with your mom as soon as her sepsis cleared up and she could walk again, you didn't get to stick around. And if you can't hang on to your lead-in audience in a prime-time slot today, it's the same thing: a little tombstone with dates on it that are heartbreakingly close together.

So how do you ensure your survival? There are two secrets to making it out there on your own. One is pretty self-evident; the other, rather less so.

SQUARE ONE

In the olden days, infant-mortality rates went down the further up the socioeconomic ladder you looked. A sickly baby born into squalid conditions to a destitute family would be doomed if it contracted, say, yellow fever. Whereas the same baby, born into a rich family of dry-goods tycoons and robber barons, would probably live as much as several days longer.

By the same token, it would appear that the more success-ful a spin-off's mother ship is, the more chance the spin-off has to survive. This seems like kind of a no-brainer; obviously, unlike poor couples, unsuccessful shows don't get spin-offs at all in the first place (unless anybody is aware of a spin-off from *Arrested Development* that escaped my attention, in which case I'd like you to spill). And big hits not only spawn more successful spin-offs, they spawn more numerous spin-offs. For instance, *The Mary Tyler Moore Show* gave birth to *Rhoda*, *Lou Grant*, and *Phyllis*. *Happy Days* launched *Laverne and Shirley*, *Mork and Mindy*, and *Joanie Loves Chachi*. On the other hand, *Three's Company*, while an undeniable hit, was not the cultural watershed those other shows are, and so it gave us . . . *The Ropers*. What this means to you and me on a practical level is that before you strike out on your own, be sure you're leaving someplace really great. Which I guess is kind of counterintuitive, but there's nothing I can do about that.

The second rule of thumb is this: *get as far away from your parents as possible*. It's a general rule that the further a spin-off goes from its source material, the better off it will be. The most obvious measure of this is geographical (which is a really good argument for moving far away from home). Very few spin-offs take place in the cities where we first met their stars. Mrs. Garrett on *The Facts of Life* started out in New York City on *Diff'rent Strokes*, for example, and on her new series she ended up in upstate New York, far enough away from the city to make it credible that snobby, ditzy Blair wasn't attacked by muggers several times a week. Frasier from *Cheers* crossed a continent in the course of spinning off, moving from Boston to Seattle in a single summer. Furthermore, in the course of the transition, he also ditched his wife, lost his mom, gained a grown brother, and brought his father back to life. Now that's putting the "spin" in "spin-off." Or maybe the "off." One of the two.

But for sheer distance, it's always going to be tough to beat the record of *Trapper John, M.D.*, who, after leaving *M*A*S*H*, put not only an entire planet but also several decades between his character's Korean War origins (technically as an Elliott Gould character in a Robert Altman film, no less) and the San Francisco hospital where he wound up as chief of surgery. The intervening years made him completely unrecognizable except for his name. The once rebellious cutup was now a more straitlaced boss type—not to mention bald, bearded, a whole lot less funny, and wholly unable to tell a story in a half hour anymore.

This was apparently a successful strategy on CBS around this time, especially for aging, bald, white actors. Lou Grant somehow made the jump from TV to print in between *The Mary Tyler Moore Show* and his eponymous spin-off, which probably makes him the only journalist in the last thirty years to do so. Most media figures prefer to do the reverse. Even more amazing was the fact that he did so in less than three weeks. His iconic departure from the WJM newsroom (as part of an amoeba-like mass that included the entire cast) was apparently powerful enough to slingshot him clear across two-thirds of the country, from Minneapolis to L.A. That's why we don't do group hugs in Minnesota anymore, in case you were wondering.

The lesson here is to make a clean break. It's inevitable, of course—especially in the early going—that the occasional visitor from home will stop by, as on *Frasier* (and he never really did shake completely free of Lilith, which probably had something to do with the fact that they had a child together), but it's to your advantage to make it as hard for them as possible. How many times did Denise Huxtable get visited by her dad once she went to Hillman College on *A Different World*? Less than once, if memory serves, and as an alumnus, he didn't even have the excuse of not knowing where the place was. Even so, Denise wasn't taking any chances, and bailed out of the show entirely as soon as she possibly could. Now, *that's* independence.

YOUR OWN PARENTS WON'T
RECOGNIZE YOU

But moving halfway across the country isn't the only way to shake your parents off. You can also become something so different from what they thought they were raising that they don't even recognize you a week after you leave. For instance, if your parents raise you as a straitlaced, family-valued, politically conservative Christian boy, it's going to come as a shock to them the first time they stop by your new place and discover that you've become, say, a woman.

The same distancing instinct seems to apply to TV spin-offs. It's amazing how many ways these series have found to depart from the things that we liked about their parent shows. For instance, people couldn't get enough of the Ewings on *Dallas,* but the ones who wound up on *Knots Landing* were pretty much the least interesting characters in that incestuous little cul-de-sac. Which isn't all that surprising, considering that Gary and Val were hardly ever on *Dallas* to begin with.

Same deal with *Melrose Place.* That was only a spin-off of *Beverly Hills 90210* in the most indirect sense, in that it was about some grown-up that Kelly had been hanging out with. But then when Jake got "his own" show, it ended up being about a whole apartment building full of Generation X-ers. To start out, they were just as boring as he was, but when permanent "special guest star" Heather Locklear joined the cast as Amanda Woodward, everyone was like, "Jake who?" Including, possibly, during the time the two of them were dating.

And we're still not done with ways to defy the parents. Back in the seventies, *The Six Million Dollar Man* was a fairly popular show about an astronaut who got wiped out in some kind of space accident, and had several key parts of his body replaced with artificial components that not only seamlessly integrated with what was left of his actual body, but were also many times stronger and more powerful than the original (a trick that modern prosthetics researchers would no doubt like to duplicate). In that show's spin-off, the star became a chick. Okay, well, Steve Austin met Jamie Sommers and dated her for a while before she took off on her own show with her robotic legs, ear, and dog. And she may not have done as well initially, but then again, *The Bionic Woman* is the one that got updated for a remake thirty-odd years later. And I don't think it was only because $6 million in the twenty-first century would barely cover a hip replacement for Steve Austin (who should be about due for one by now anyway).

Of course it can be tempting in the short term to maintain close relations with your parents (or parent show), as *Angel* did. Comfortably ensconced for its first two seasons in the time slot after its progenitor, *Buffy*, *Angel* was almost like a weekly sequel to each *Buffy* episode. *Angel* also had the added benefit of not one but two (and later three) regular characters who originated on *Buffy*. Plus there was the constant promise of getting to see other *Buffy* characters in any given *Angel* episode, like Willow, Harmony, Faith, Andrew, and, oh yeah, Buffy. It kept people tuning in for a while, but *Angel* only lasted one sad season after the end of *Buffy*, parading the cold comfort of Spike around, despite his most recent death in the *Buffy* finale. Buffy herself only made one more brief appearance in *Angel's* last season, but she was played by a different actor shot only from the back. So from this we can draw a clear lesson: when you move out, move out. Don't just move next door, and for God's sake don't claim all of the old furniture and carpet that your parents put out on their curb. That isn't going to make their friends come and see you.

THIS TOWN AIN'T BIG ENOUGH
FOR ALL OF US

So what happens if you ignore my advice and stick around in the same town as your parents? Well, let's compare a couple of similar TV-show families and find out.

New York is, by all accounts, a fairly large city. You'd think there'd be plenty of space for a whole dreary litter of *Law & Order* kittens to coexist peacefully. But the reality has proved somewhat different. *Law & Order: There's Nothing Original About It Anymore at This Point* spun off *Law & Order: Sex Police* and *Law & Order: Vincent D'Onofrio Is Batshit Crazy*, and hardly had to recycle any of the cast. Because of these shows, most of the world probably thinks that New York City has three district attorneys at any given time. And it hasn't all gone smoothly. There was also *Law & Order: Trial by Jury*,, which kept Jerry Orbach as Detective Lennie Briscoe from the original *Law & Order*. Both show and actor suffered a swift death. Furthermore, as of this writing, there is talk of canceling the original *L&O* outright, as there are no actors left in New York who have not already been on it. Worse yet, one of the spin-offs was temporarily exiled to a nonbroadcast network to hang out with Adrian Monk, Shawn Spencer, and Michael Westen.[1] For a grown child, that's like the equivalent of moving into a college dorm.

CSI, on the other hand, booted its chicks as far out of the nest as they could fly. The Las Vegas–set mother ship could have gone the *Law & Order* route and engendered a spin-off about the Clark County Crime Lab's day shift, or about Vegas cops who carried heat instead of little collection envelopes. But instead, they helped the kids set up housekeeping in Miami and New York, and all three shows are doing fine. Better than *Law & Order: Can We Come Back to NBC?* is, that's for sure.

MOVING BACK HOME

You may occasionally find yourself fantasizing about having your parents' house to yourself after they're gone (whether it be to the nursing home, Florida, or syndication). It's a tempting dream. You get your very own digs, but you already know where everything is and how everything works, and you can even start changing some things that have been bugging you about the place. Who wouldn't be drawn to that scenario? One drawback: it's a trap. You'll die there. And fast.

At least that's what we can surmise by looking at the spin-offs of shows that take over the same time slot that their now-canceled parent shows once occupied. That's what happened

---

1. See the "Private Eyes" section of chapter 7, "Don't Do the Crime If You Can't Do the Time."

with *After M*A*S*H*. Apparently CBS figured that of the three people in the universe who had failed to not only watch but even hear about *M*A*S*H*'s thirteen-hour finale the prior spring, one or two of them might not be too eagle-eyed to notice that the Korean War setting had moved to a Stateside hospital, all but three of the most boring cast members were gone, and Klinger had given up his old wardrobe of dresses for a considerably gayer-looking collection of argyle sweater vests. Alas, notice they did. And subsequently stopped watching.

More or less the same thing happened with *Joey*, the sad attempt to keep the love of *Friends* alive Thursdays at eight o'clock Eastern. Then there are those shows that try to seamlessly morph into something new, the way *All in the Family* became the sad, shambling revenant of a TV show that was *Archie Bunker's Place*. Somehow, in the process of becoming a widower and a bar owner, that hateful old bigot turned into a mushy pushover who did things like take in orphans. When we all know that the old Archie would have left the kid on the steps of the police station in a basket. Never mind that she was nearly ten years old at the time.

It's even worse when the stars of a spin-off try to come home again. After the brief run of *The X-Files* spin-off *The Lone Gunmen* came to its end, the three title characters returned to *The X-Files* for an episode in which all of them were killed. Next to that, suddenly coming home from college to find your old bedroom turned into a home entertainment center doesn't seem so bad.

And look at what *Three's Company* became, when Jack Tripper moved out of his apartment with Janet and whichever dizzy blonde was living there that month, gave up his philandering ways, and devoted himself to one woman. I don't even remember what that show was called, it disappeared so quickly. In fact, I might even be thinking about how Fonzie ended up on *Happy Days*.

CONCLUSION

Leaving home can be a frightening proposition, especially now that you know that it can't be done halfway. But as scary as it may be to change every aspect of your life at once, it's really the best way to ensure your success. Changing jobs or even careers is all well and good, but if you really want to pull this off, you're also going to need to be willing to move at least half-way across the country, make all new friends, spend a few years or decades in suspended animation, and possibly even change what kind of person you are, including your gender. There, I hope I've made the prospect of life changes a lot less stressful for you.

Learning Experiences

1 Think of your life's inner circle—your group of friends, co-workers, family, tangential acquaintances, whatever. Decide which of them is most deserving of their own spin-off. Then buy them a plane ticket.

2 Most of us have been through at least one major life change that would qualify as a spin-off for a television character. Think about your most recent one, and whether your life was better before or after. If it was better before, see if the original environment will take you back. Actually, don't bother—it won't.

3 Change jobs, move across the country, and start hanging out with completely different people than you used to, as abruptly as possible. You may wish to hold off on this one until just after you have completed experience number two in Chapter 7 and committed a crime.

4 Decide that a current show is a spin-off of another show (the older the initial show, the better), even if it isn't. Start an urban myth that it is.

14

Listen Attentively,
I Mean About Future Calamity

The Final Chapter

Most of us think of death as something that happens only to other people. And it's easy to understand why; all our lives, it only *has* happened to other people. Let's face it, if it had ever happened to you, you probably wouldn't be reading this right now. But there's no way around it: someday death will come for you, and then *you'll* be other people.

THE BEGINNING OF THE END

It's not much different on television. Who are the characters you spend the most time with, the ones you feel closest to? The leads, of course; the regulars, the people who show up every week, the ones who have their names and faces in the opening credits. They hardly ever die, and even when they do, it might not completely "take."

Whereas you learn early on not to get too attached to people who aren't in the opening credits. On the original *Star Trek,* when Kirk, Spock, McCoy, and an unfamiliar security officer in a familiar red shirt beamed down to the alien planet, it wasn't going to be the security officer who ultimately called back, "Three to beam up." Although it's considered one of TV's great injustices that the original *Star Trek* only lasted seventy-eight episodes, Kirk's initial crew of 432 was already dangerously depleted by the end of the series. And the spectacle of the *Enterprise* being run by a skeleton crew of a dozen or so along about year eight of the five-year mission would have been even more embarrassing than the episode entitled "Spock's Brain."

So, sure, guest stars and extras die off like mayflies, on that show and many others. Sometimes, that's their entire purpose. Even well-known faces aren't safe; on *ER,* the more famous a guest star is, the less likely they are to get out of County General alive. They'll hang around long enough to touch the hearts of the regular cast, and then it's all codes and crash carts and circling cameras and a can with an Emmy reel in it. This should serve as a warning to all health-care workers, everywhere: if a celebrity ever shows up at your facility, stay well clear. Because when he or she dies, you don't want to be around.

But regular lead characters on television series don't often kick off, and when they do, it's kind of a big deal. For decades, TV action shows have been trying to convince us that the star or a dear sidekick is in mortal danger week in and week out. Of course we know they're going to get out of it. The only question is how, and how much of a strain on our credulity it'll be.

TV also proves again and again that the only time a star is ever in real danger is if his contract is up. Then all bets are off. For example, in 1975, when McLean Stevenson left *M*A*S*H,* his character, Lieutenant Colonel Henry Blake, had finished his tour of duty and was on his way home from the Korean War. And then the doctors he left behind at the 4077th got word that the plane carrying him home had been shot down. No survivors. Viewers were shocked.

Oh, come *on.* Sure, it's sad and all, but he was leaving the show anyway. What are the stakes in killing off a character who's already left? When you don't get to see the final scene? Really, the only impact on the show is that a) the remaining characters act sad, and b) it's just that much more unlikely that the actor who played the deceased character will be returning for a guest spot. A contract expiration is never going to lead to a very surprising demise.

It was a similar story with the long-running and misnomered *Good Times.* That show hardly ever left the Evanses' apartment, and showing us a car crash would have been as far outside its scope as, well, any other scene set outdoors. But when patriarch James Evans became a vehicular fatality on the eve of the family's move to Atlanta, it was hard not to feel gypped at getting the news, along with the rest of the family, by telegram.[1]

At least the eighties yuppie drama *thirtysomething* got a little

1. Kudos are to be given to John Amos, whose death scene on *The West Wing* years later was much more spectacular, when, as Admiral Fitzwallace, he got his Joint Chiefs chairman ass blown up good by a car bomb in Gaza.

more creative. Nancy spent a season battling cancer, complete with baroque, death-centered fantasy sequences that featured coffin lids slamming on her face and everything. And then came the episode where she entered the hospital for the last time. ABC promised a death that hour, but Nancy pulled through. And then *bam,* cyclist Gary got creamed by a truck. The lesson? Even when you see death coming, it's still likely to have a few surprises up its big black sleeve.

Except that Gary didn't die on-screen, which, again, lessened the impact. Worse yet, his ghost kept showing up to give Michael advice. That's no kind of killing, especially on *thirtysomething.* Sure, he only existed inasmuch as Michael continued to perceive him, but that was true of every other character on the show, anyway.

These prime-time deaths, however, occurred in a more innocent era. Eventually, death became less of a surprise and more of a teary, treacly ratings stunt, like those of Bobby Simone on *N.Y.P.D. Blue* or Dr. Mark Greene on *ER*. At least they died on-screen, so that was an improvement, but both were billed as "a hero's farewell." That's a little tough to relate to. Most people don't get a hero's farewell—at least not people who watch as much TV as you and I do.

But death of one sort or another is getting closer. To all of us. It's inevitable. That stark fact is reflected in the television of the last ten years. A decade ago, leading TV characters were simply a lot less likely to die on us than they are now. That's because—and, I'm sorry, but there's no polite way to say this—so were you.

DEAD OR UNDEAD?

Unsurprisingly, a clear starting point for this trend (as with so many others) was *Buffy the Vampire Slayer*. How apropos that a series dealing with creatures from beyond the grave was also one of the first prime-time shows to break taboos regarding the death of major characters. Including, in more than one instance, the lead character.

Of course the rules are always different when you're dealing with the undead. From the very start, it was clear that death (and undeath) was going to play a major part in this story. And not just because a kid got eaten by a vampire in the first scene of the first episode. When you're in high school, everything seems like a life-or-death issue. At Sunnydale High, everything *was*. The pilot episode even introduced a character the writers tried to pass off as a regular, but who then got killed in the first hour.[2] Clearly it sucks to live over a Hellmouth.

Buffy also taught us that when you take risks and do the right thing, well, sometimes it gets you killed. Even if you're the star. In the first-season finale, a prophecy came to light stating that Buffy was going to die. The episode did a great job of building a sense of hopeless foreboding, even against the powerful juju of Buffy's being the star of the series. But of course Buffy would be safe, we told ourselves. How silly of us to worry. And then she died.

Yes, Xander and Buffy's vampire boyfriend Angel (who, strictly speaking, had *already* been dead for centuries) quickly

---

2. "Jesse," played by Eric Balfour.

brought her back with mouth-to-mouth,[3] which made the following six seasons possible. But we'll come back to that in a minute. In any case, the message was clear: nobody is safe.

And death on *Buffy* wasn't always temporary or even supernatural. The episode "The Body," which dealt with the aftermath of the death of Buffy's mom by natural causes, was as educational a portrayal of grief as you'll ever see on television. When you lose someone close to you, your whole life seems to stop. The trajectory of the season's storyline (and the music, and the wisecracks, and the wacky editing) grinds to a halt and all the scenes are really long and all the camera angles are subtly off-kilter, at least until something snaps you out of it, like having to fight a newly risen vampire in the morgue next to your dead mom's gurney. And the battle will be ugly and brutal and will only serve to show that even when someone close to you dies, your life still goes on. Especially if your life is about killing vampires.

YOUR TIME HAS COME

Time marches on, and time and death go hand in hand. And if the time on a given show is "real," what does that say about death on that same show?

24 should have died itself a long time ago. For one thing, its format is built around the gimmick of "real time." It was marketed as the story of "one unforgettable day," which sounded like a pretty clearly stated mandate for a single-season drama. In keeping up the pace for twenty-four episodes, without the abil-

---

3. Which didn't seem like as much of a cheat as it could have been in light of the fact that most ancient prophecies predate CPR.

ity to flash back, zip past boring parts, or even allow characters time to go to the bathroom, the creators set themselves up with a difficult challenge: who in the viewing audience would want to work that hard to keep up with such a rigorously chronological show, anyway?

Thus the structure of season one reflects the ongoing threat of an early death to the show itself. For the first twelve hours, Agent Jack Bauer is primarily occupied with preventing the murder of his kidnapped wife and daughter by villain Ira Gaines. During the season's twelfth episode, Jack single-handedly storms the kidnappers' compound, frees his family, and kills Gaines. It's an episode widely recognized as one of the show's best. They say you should live each day as though it were your last. This episode was written as though it was *24*'s last, and it was a knockout as a result. If only the show hadn't been picked up for the full season, let alone six or seven or thirty-eight more, it wouldn't have gone downhill. Maybe that was the problem: it may or may not be a good idea to live every day as if it's your last, but if you only live one day that way, the ones that follow are going to be kind of a letdown.

Still, as much as one might complain about each season being worse than the last (and a lot more than one have), one thing has remained fairly consistent about the show throughout its run, and that is its body count.

Just to drive this point home, let's take a look at the original "regular" cast of *24*. In addition to protagonist Jack Bauer, there was his wife, Teri, and daughter, Kim. At the office, he interacted with bosses Mason and Chappelle, as well as underlings Nina, Tony, and Milo.[4] For much of the season, he was trying

---

4. Milo was played by Eric Balfour.

to thwart attempts on the life of Senator David Palmer, who in turn had his hands full with his ambitious wife, Sherry.

So that's ten people. As of this writing, eight of those characters have been killed off. On-screen, in most cases. Six of them were fatally shot, while Mason perished spectacularly in a nuclear explosion. And an eighth (Tony) barely survived a car bombing that killed his wife, only to be killed by a suspect hours later.[5] Any way you look at it, 24 is a dangerous place to be.

But it's a veritable day-care center compared to a certain other show I could (and will) mention, where you could count on someone failing to survive the first scene of every episode.

CAN YOU DIG IT?

TV taught me how to dress for funerals, so imagine my surprise the first time I showed up at one and was the only person in a black suit and black tie. I guess by age seventeen, I should have known better. Up until that time, at most of the funerals I'd been to, the best-dressed person in attendance was in the casket. Pretty much everyone else seemed to be dressed for a business meeting, or for a regular church service, rather than a TV funeral, where everyone seems to have the same tailor and the widow gets to wear a chic veiled hat of the kind I've never once seen in person outside of school plays.

There was also the issue of how much longer funerals last in real life than they do on TV, which struck me as a bitter irony; just at this time when we are all by definition faced with the reality of

---

5. We'll be coming back to that as well.

our own mortality, here we are stuck in a pew for an hour or more, right when we'd most like to be getting on with the business of living. And of all the funerals I've encountered, the only ones at which I've heard the Twenty-third Psalm recited ("Yea, though I walk through the valley of the shadow of death," etc.) are the ones I've seen on TV (and for the record, I want the verse from Ezekiel that Samuel L. Jackson recites in *Pulp Fiction* read at mine).

But put yourself for a moment in the funeral director's shiny black shoes. Chances are he'll be much more messed up than you, at least on the inside. That's what we learned from the "groundbreaking" (get it?) drama *Six Feet Under*, which taught us that the end was always just the beginning, and that death is really about the ones left behind.

After all, what could put death more in your face than a show about a family that owned a funeral parlor? Created by Alan Ball (who at the time was most famous for having written the Oscar-winning film *American Beauty*, a movie narrated by a dead guy), *Six Feet Under* took an unflinching look at death every single week.

We all know that death is certain in the long term. But in *Six Feet Under*'s darkly ironic opening scenes, death is certain within the next five minutes. At least one guest player per week opened the episode by meeting a grisly end right out of a *Final Destination* movie. From the woman who ran into traffic after seeing a truckload of helium-filled sex dolls escaping skyward and thinking the rapture had come, to the woman who discovered that limousine moon roofs and low bridges are a dangerous combination, to the guy who accidentally ran over himself in his driveway, death constantly proved random, unpredictable, and *always* ready for its moment. But how does knowing that help us? I'm sorry, but all I can really tell you is that if you ever happen to hear the *Six Feet Under* opening theme song out of nowhere, just lie down, cover your head, and wait for the danger to pass. By which I mean, let someone else get taken out.

Of course all of this death was rather hard on the series lead, Nate Fisher. He had grown up in his father's funeral home but, as soon as he was legally able, left home to find a new life where he wouldn't have to sleep in a house with corpses in the basement. But after Nathaniel Sr. died in the pilot, Nate had to return to run the family business—in other words, confront the reality of death, the inevitability of death, the unpredictability of death, and the *grossness* of death, every damn day. "I'm slipping in a guy's guts here," he once observed in horror, teaching us that we never, ever want to be a funeral director. Sometimes it was almost like watching *Monk*, but with a lead character who was constantly coming face to face with his same, single phobia instead of bucketloads of them.

Having to usher others into the next life for a living was bad enough for Nate, but it got worse when he was diagnosed with a potentially deadly and deeply symbolic brain condition that could literally kill him at any moment. And that also served to warn us all that really, *any* of us could die at any moment, brain condition or no.[6]

And it didn't help that Nate turned out to be almost as dangerous a guy to know as Jack Bauer. In the course of five seasons, he experienced the deaths of his father, his wife, his brother-in-law, his unborn child, his little sister's boyfriend,[7] a high school buddy,

6. Are you still there? You're all right? Okay, just checking.

7. "Gabe," played by Eric Balfour. Is he kidding us with this shit?

and his first lover. Really, with a guy like that, the only responsible thing is for somebody to take him out. Fortunately, in the last-but-three episode, his brain condition finally did just that.

But *Six Feet Under*, being *Six Feet Under*, wasn't satisfied with killing off just one regular character. At the end of the series finale, the show flashed forward to the deaths of every single cast member. It took some doing—little sister Claire, the youngest, lasted another eighty years—but *Six Feet Under* wouldn't rest until all of its characters were resting in peace. Don't hold your breath waiting for a reunion episode. Because you'll die.

ASK NOT FOR WHOM THE BELL TOLLS

TV teaches us that death is a lot more likely now than it used to be (which is the opposite of what science teaches us, but this isn't a science book). In recent years, death itself has almost become a recurring character all over the dial. The more serialized a show, the more dangerous it is for the characters who populate it. Recent shows like *Lost* and *Prison Break* kill off regular characters almost as quickly as they introduce them. Even teen-centered soaps aren't safe, as viewers of *The O.C.* learned when that show's female lead was killed off at the end of the third season. That, of course, probably had something to do with Marissa Cooper's unpopularity. But even that move didn't save *The O.C.* itself from death.

It's getting to the point where it's more unusual for a show to *not* kill off characters. Regular cast members have taken dirt naps on *Heroes*, *Desperate Housewives*, *CSI: Miami*, and any number of other current shows that life is too short to mention. In fact, despite the notoriously high body count on *Battlestar Galactica*, that show was starting to get some grief about having never killed off a before-the-credits character. This despite the fact that Baltar's imaginary Cylon girlfriend *was already dead*. Still, near the end of the third season, *B*G* picked its way through the mass grave that already contained Admiral Adama's younger son, Colonel Tigh's wife, the president's chief of staff, Admiral Cain, and any number of Cylons several times over (including series regular Sharon), and killed off Starbuck. The producers of the 1970s version of the series would have killed themselves before they let that happen.

ARISE

Death is supposed to be final. The end of the line. The undiscovered country from which no man returneth,[8] or whatever. Whoever says that doesn't own a TV.

Because let's face it, some characters don't exactly stay dead, do they? Years after her first death, Buffy sacrificed her life to save that of her sister, even though said sister was a) an artificial construct, and b) annoying. This time, she stayed dead all summer, until her friends concocted a spell to bring her back. Buffy literally clawed her way out of her grave, but was never quite the same; to borrow an expression from Stephen King's *Pet Sematary*, Buffy—and, in a sense, *Buffy*—"came back wrong." Yes, the last two seasons never lived up to the ones that had gone before, and we all learned not to trifle with death.

---

8. *Star Trek VI: The Undiscovered Country*. Act II, Scene iv.

Okay, *some* of us did. Whereas on *Six Feet Under* there were still three episodes to kill (if you'll pardon the expression) when the show's lead character kicked off. But as always with *Six Feet Under,* the end was only the beginning. From episode one, the deceased would never just lie quietly on the slab; it became their job to be really, really honest with you. So like Nate's father and so many Fisher "clients" before him, Nate reappeared to everyone in his life—helping David conquer his panic disorder; spewing a bunch of drugged-out but somehow helpful hippie nonsense to Claire to help her overcome her fear of the future; and helping Brenda get past her incestuous feelings about her brother and come to terms with being a single mom—in order to solve their problems. And it was a good thing too, because really, there *were* only three episodes left.

Even the starkly realistic-looking *Battlestar Galactica* isn't immune, as human-appearing Cylons have the ability, upon death, to download their minds into an identical new body and return unscathed, which spares producers the trouble of recasting their roles. And what of the many actual human characters who have been done away with? Well, the late Starbuck returned in a season-finale episode, not looking all that dead at all. Of course at this point in that same episode, everyone watching was still too confused (if not enraged) about aliens who didn't even know where Earth was—let alone had ever been there—and having auditory hallucinations of "All Along the Watchtower" to worry too much about what it all meant.

The list goes on. Mary Alice Young has been dead for years but still shows up every week to superciliously narrate *Desperate Housewives.* Tim Speedle came back to *CSI: Miami,* an oddly paranormal occurrence for a show that's ostensibly about scientists.

The Petrelli brothers literally exploded in a nuclear detonation on *Heroes* yet turned up again, damaged but alive, four months later. Dead characters on *Lost* keep reappearing in flashbacks. And even on *24*, one of the aforementioned dead characters, Tony, was brought back to life in season seven. Producers made the excuse that in Tony's "death" scene two years before, there was no "silent clock" to close out the act, as usually happens to mark the (frequent) deaths of major characters on that show. In the same way that soap-opera fans have been trained not to believe anyone's dead until they see the body, *24* fans now know not to believe anyone's dead without a silent clock.

So clearly, death isn't as permanent as we may have been led to believe. But how is it determined who stays behind the veil, and who returns? Wiser men than I have struggled with this question. But I'm thinking that being really popular with the viewers couldn't possibly hurt.

And now there are whole shows about returning from the dead. *Pushing Daisies* is a whimsical comedy about a pie-maker who can touch dead people and bring them back to life. But then if he touches them again, they die again, this time for good (supposedly). And then there's the show about the guy whose soul is owned by the devil, so he has to walk the earth pursuing damned souls who have escaped from hell so that they can be returned to their eternal punishment. This show, which premiered in 1998, was called *Brimstone* and met an early death of its own. But in 2007 it escaped from the TV underworld with a reworked plot, a completely new cast, and a diametrically opposed atmosphere, as well as a new title: *Reaper*. Most mortals don't recognize it from its previous incarnation, but I do. Please don't ask me how.

I will say this, however. At this point, I believe that there's only one character on all of series TV whom the creators will never dare to resurrect after a dramatic death scene: Maude Flanders on *The Simpsons*. It would be just too unrealistic.

MEMENTO MORI (CONCLUSION)

We all like to think we're immortal. We all like to think our loved ones are immortal, and that our favorite TV characters are immortal. But we're not, and they're not. If the evolution of death on television over the past thirty years has shown us anything, it's that death is getting closer. In fact, it's closer to you than it was yesterday. How much closer can it get without actually reaching out of the TV and killing us like something from *The Ring*?

Well, there was a show called *Dead Like Me*, which purported to explore what it was like to actually be dead. But I can't tell you much about it, because that show is, well, dead.

Learning Experiences

1 Attend an actual funeral. Bring along a portable DVD player or a video iPod or something loaded with a funeral scene from a television show. See how many times you can watch the scene during the actual funeral (for safety's sake, have someone else drive you from the funeral home to the cemetery).

2 Regardless of your age, imagine how your life would be different if one out of every ten people you know died once a year. In

order to best experience this hypothetical situation, you should actually cut that person off for good. No need to explain to them why—they're dead.

3 Ask around to see if anybody you know has ever known someone to return from the dead. Check workplaces, schools, social functions, and churches.

4 Die. Not right now; just whenever you get around to it.

AFTERWORD

Together, we've learned a lot from TV. But *learning from* TV is just the beginning. At some point in your life, perhaps soon, perhaps even already, you may find yourself in a position where you're responsible for the molding of a young mind. And then it will fall to you to *teach with* TV.

This is an awesome responsibility. Fortunately, the parents, teachers, day-care providers, and juvenile corrections officers of today have tools at their disposal that previous generations did not. Some of us remember growing up making do with what we could learn from public television and *Howdy Doody* and *Schoolhouse Rock*. But the multiplicity of children's cable channels, videos, and DVDs currently available make it possible to stick a flailing blob with a fresh umbilical stump in front of a TV and then, eighteen years and an indeterminate number of diaper changes later, unlock the door to the spare bedroom and release an articulate (if smart-alecky) adult who's just one long shower away from becoming a fully functioning member of society.

But I exaggerate. I don't mean to say that parents can entirely abdicate the responsibility of raising their children. The TV can't do it all. You need to familiarize yourself with how to lock certain channels, and maybe look into this V-chip we've been vaguely hearing about for what seems like forever. Most importantly, there's one thing the TV can never teach your child, and that's how to operate the remote. They can jerk it at the TV as hard as the people *in* the TV do, but that won't help them master the subtleties and nuances of fast-forwarding through the ads, let alone picture-in-picture. Maybe *their* children will have access to technology that will help them manage these tools instinctively, but for now a bit more parental involvement is called for.

But that's okay. Children are the future, and one day they can look back nostalgically, even gratefully, on the times you spent together on the couch. Not as gratefully as the times you weren't on the couch and had forgotten to lock those channels I mentioned earlier, but we can't be with them every second. And given the dreck kids like to watch—over and over and over— who would want to, really?

In the end, like any educational tool, television is only as good as the person who wields it. And remember, as you teach and raise your children or students or clients or underage detainees, that their future is in your hands. So it's only fair that once in a while, the remote should be as well.

ACKNOWLEDGMENTS

There are any number of people without whom this book would not exist, or at least be a whole lot worse. My agent, Kate Epstein, never gave up on finding a home for the idea, and my editor, Shannon Jamieson Vazquez, never gave up on making the manuscript the best it could be (much as I might have secretly wished on occasion that she would). Tara Ariano, Sarah Bunting, and Dave Cole at Television Without Pity hired me to write funny stuff about TV in the first place, and the site's stellar staff has been showing us all how that's done for most of a decade. None more so than Linda Holmes, who also helped guide me through the experiences of a first-time author trying to propose and market a nonfiction book.

Thanks are also due to the past, present, and future readers of my weblog, Velcrometer. I'm also grateful to my family and friends, especially my sisters, Renee and Rachelle, and my parents, Darrell and Rosemary Alexander, who encouraged my writing while I was growing up and taught me even more than TV did. And also to Garrison Keillor and the staff of Prairie Home Productions, who made me a professional writer (with invaluable assistance in getting there from Irene Rossman). I also owe thanks to my son, Max, and his birth parents, who made it possible for me to write this book's parenting chapter from something other than total ignorance. But most of all I am indebted to my wife, Lora, without whose support and courage I would be nowhere. Seriously, I'd be, like, in a hole someplace.

Oh, and also to the people who write, make, and watch TV.

A former staff writer for public radio's *A Prairie Home Companion* with Garrison Keillor, **Jeff Alexander** writes about TV for the popular website Television Without Pity. He lives in Minneapolis with his wife and son. Visit his own award-winning website at www.velcrometer .blogspot.com.

Printed in the United States
by Baker & Taylor Publisher Services